JOHN SAMWAYS

GOD'S
FINGERPRINTS

THE EVIDENCE IS EVERYWHERE

'These are written that you may believe…'

John 20:31

Matador
9 Priory Business Park,
Wistow Road, Kibworth Beauchamp,
Leicestershire. LE8 0RX
Tel: 0116 279 2299
Email: books@troubador.co.uk
Web: www.troubador.co.uk/matador
Twitter: @matadorbooks

ISBN 978 1784623 982

British Library Cataloguing in Publication Data.
A catalogue record for this book is available from the British Library.

Printed and bound in the UK by TJ International, Padstow, Cornwall
Typeset in Aldine by Troubador Publishing Ltd, Leicester, UK

Matador is an imprint of Troubador Publishing Ltd

To my fellow collaborators in the journey of life – Chris, Roger and Lucy, Jo and Nick, Dylan, Phoebe, Poppy and Harry. I am hugely indebted to each of you for your loving tolerance of my obsessive preoccupations, your constant encouragement and your desire to share life in all its fullness.

Acknowledgements

I am deeply grateful to Chris for her patient reading and reflection on the text, to Su Box for her advice and editorial help, and to Tony Grady for the illustrations.

'"We live on a visited planet." John Samways concludes this gentle and encouraging book with these words. Entertaining, readable and above all convincing, John offers real life stories of the way God leaves his fingerprints all about us, working in and through our ordinary lives – often when we least expect it!'

Revd Dr Alison Morgan
Author of A Wild Gospel, *Monarch*

'It's brilliant! I'm so glad John has managed to get round to writing these remarkable stories down, they are such a source of encouragement, and I often feel they connect more with people's lives than the accounts of extraordinary miracles...'

Revd Canon David MacInnes
Former Rector, St Aldates Church, Oxford

'The writing is very immediate and from the heart, gathered together in such an interesting and unusual way. A delight.'

Mary Colwell
Award-winning TV and radio producer, writer and environmentalist. Author of John Muir: The Scotsman who saved America's wild places, *Lion Hudson*

'The entire book flows out of a meticulous attentiveness to life and authentic love for other people which creates compelling contexts for the Divine finger to paint its artwork in people's lives. This is a winsomely wooing book that is all about living by faith amidst the seeming chaos of life. It should be taken as medicine by those who suffer from "practical atheism"!'

Charles Nienkirchen
Professor of Christian History and Spirituality at Ambrose University College, Calgary, Canada

'What was it Jesus said about having eyes to see and ears to hear? Read John Samways' stories and find the scales falling from one's eyes. What encouraging tales. Time and again he shows us evidence of God at work in the little things... as well as the big panoramic sweep. My favourite is 'Budgerigar', perhaps because I've also glimpsed God working in the lives of older people whose pet birds are a particular source of companionship and consolation.'

Debbie Thrower, former broadcaster and team leader of BRF's The Gift of Years: resourcing the spiritual journey of older people, and their first Anna Chaplain

'Stories have become the most effective way of communicating truth and there are very compelling and meaningful stories here, each linked with a number of interesting historical and etymological facts, and scripture.'

Revd Canon Michael Mitton
Author, Fresh Expressions Officer for the Diocese of Derby

'I am excited by this book. These stories, culled from over 50 years of wide and fascinating experience are guaranteed to grab you, and show the excitement this sports-mad former vicar has in being a follower of Jesus and introducing others to him. You can start reading these short stories wherever a title catches your eye. Buy it and give it to your sceptical friends!'

Revd Canon Dr Michael Green
Theologian, writer

CONTENTS

PREFACE

When will we come to our senses? This is an important question. Humans are blessed to varying degrees with five senses which we recognise and deeply value: sight, hearing, smell, touch and taste. However there are intuitive senses which are equally vital yet all too often unrecognised and unappreciated. They work together and offer us a series of ancient 'tools' to help us navigate through life. Our senses bestow upon each of us a capacity for awareness, both of revealing who we are and what (or who) is 'out there', and the phrase 'coming to our senses' really means waking up to what is. As a species we call ourselves Homo sapiens sapiens, an anatomically modern human sub species of Homo sapiens (*sapiens* is a Latin word meaning 'wise'), which means that potentially we possess a double dose of *knowing* through sensing and the activity of the mind.

Yet we need to realise how little we actually see, hear,

smell, taste or feel. Yes, we do a lot of looking, and yet for years we can walk down the same street and never quite 'see' it. We 'lose sight' of much that is happening around us. Similarly, we can so easily be 'out of touch' not only with the sense of touch but with other senses too. We really *do* need to come to all our senses!

It is fascinating that of all the senses, in the *Oxford English Dictionary* 'touch' is the longest entry (far longer than even 'love'), because touch is so basic to life – 'with touch you know you know'. The only way we know anything is by 'touching' it *through* our senses. Touching is reciprocal; you cannot touch without being touched and when we allow ourselves to register we are being touched, a new relational, deeper 'knowing' arises and we become more fully alive.

In the midst of the soul-numbing gallop of modern times, is it possible to detect the touch of God upon our lives? Surely, if God *is* God and is living up to his name of Emmanuel, which means 'God with us', should we not *expect* him to touch our lives?

The stories in this book seek to answer this question. The evidence of God's touch can be found everywhere along the journey of a commonplace life.

One touch can change everything!

'Moses said, "Now show me your glory."'

Exodus 33:18

INTRODUCTION

> **Fingerprint** (a dictionary definition)
> Noun: an impression of the markings of the inner surface of the last joint of the thumb or other finger.
> - such an impression made with ink for purposes of identification.
> - any unique or distinctive pattern that represents unambiguous evidence of a specific person etc.
> Verb: to take or record the fingerprints of.

Fingerprints are recognised as an inescapable mark of identity and have been for generations. There is archaeological evidence that they were used as signatures in ancient Babylon, 4,000 years ago, and the oldest fingerprint discovered dates from the Neolithic period in north-western China 6,000 years ago.

Following the invention of the microscope in the early seventeenth century, largely the work of Galileo, more detailed observations could be made of the human skin and in due time it was discovered that, like snowflakes, each person's fingerprint is unique. Even Siamese twins have unique fingerprints! This discovery led to the use of fingerprint evidence in criminal investigation.

The first criminal case in which fingerprint evidence was used to secure conviction was in Bengal in 1898 and the first trial decided by fingerprints in an English court, a case of aggravated burglary, was in 1902. Following the advent of computers, the ability to store forensic evidence worldwide increased exponentially and fingerprints are now the most commonly gathered data, providing an inescapable mark of identity.

The symbol of fingerprints is a resonant one in terms of ownership, perhaps of a political policy or the style of play of a team – for example, 'that tax bill had the Chancellor's fingerprints all over it'. It is in this sense that these stories seek to reveal how God's 'fingerprints' can be found in the midst of our daily lives.

This book recounts incidents and situations from the four decades of my life after becoming a Christian at the age of thirty-one. Some years previously, having been brought up in a church-going family, but with no sense of the need to make a personal commitment to God, I had turned away from my faith journey. It happened in a dramatic fashion.

It was Christmas Eve 1965 and at 11.00 p.m. I walked into my local church, which I had attended since childhood, to participate in the Midnight Mass. I was in my final year at university and had returned home for the Christmas vacation filled with anticipation at the prospect of meeting up with old school friends and neighbours.

As I entered the building the familiar smell of church antiquity and the accompanying warm welcome made me feel immediately 'at home' and I settled down, waiting for the service to begin. In the course of the following hour and a half, I cannot remember precisely how or when it happened, I discovered that I was suddenly aware, in a blinding and inescapable way, that although I felt so at home in the surroundings I did not believe the truths lying at the heart of Christian doctrine. This was much more than mere doubt. Rather, it could only be likened to a 'reverse conversion experience' and I found it immediately and deeply disturbing: so much so that as I walked out of church that night into Christmas Day, I vowed that I would 'never go into a church for the rest of my life'. Atheism was on my lips and in my heart.

I still recall vividly the sense of shock that I felt at the totally unexpected, sudden loss of a hitherto largely unquestioned belief system. However, the demands of quickly approaching final exams and the need for decisions to be taken regarding my post-university activities meant that I had little time on my hands to ponder deep questions. That time was to present itself in the coming year when I embarked upon a year in Nigeria as a volunteer, serving with Voluntary Service Overseas (VSO).

Following that Christmas Eve experience, it was many years before I became a Christian, years in which I was unconsciously exploring my faith journey. Usually this exploration happened in an incidental way, amid the daily challenges of life as a newly married geography teacher, sports enthusiast and father of two young children. Over the course of those years I began to recognise that my newfound position of atheism was being challenged – challenged by what I would now identify as 'fingerprints' of God, but then often saw as inconvenient interruptions in the daily cycle of life; inconvenient because they raised some uncomfortable questions. 'What is the ultimate goal in life?' 'What does it mean to lead a good life?' 'Is there life after death?' 'Why is there such suffering and evil in the world? and many more.

These questions have occupied the minds of great philosophers for centuries and continue to do so. My coming to faith in Jesus Christ did not simply resolve them all for me, I still have many unanswered questions, but I discovered that the knowledge of a personal relationship with God and Christian doctrine offer a framework and perspective within which the questions of life, big and small, can be addressed. I found a new direction, purpose and hope in life.

Each story that follows shows how the 'fingerprints' of God can be found in the living of life, invariably in totally unexpected ways. Just as it is recognised that a fingerprint is only a fraction of the whole being it represents, in the same way none of the stories is presented as the 'final answer' to the big questions about life and God. Yet in each story there are glimpses of the hand of God and his values and, as 'evidence' is gathered, the identity of the one responsible for the prints becomes clearer.

Some stories will resonate more clearly than others with the reader, depending upon the interests, passions and circumstances of each individual. Choose one story initially, the title of which arouses your curiosity for some reason, and then continue your journey through the book, reading the stories in whatever order you wish.

Perhaps the stories will help you to discover the fingerprints of God upon your own journey of life.

> 'The basic reality of God is plain enough. Open your eyes and there it is!'
>
> *Romans 1:20*, The Message

AUNT SALLY

'Stay open to opportunity – you never know when your next important connection will be made.'

Nicholas Boothman

Aunt Sally is a traditional throwing game dating back at least as far as the seventeenth century. Introduced to Oxford by Royalist soldiers during the English Civil War when King Charles set up court in the city, Aunt Sally is still played as a pub game in Oxfordshire, Warwickshire, Berkshire and Buckinghamshire. The 10-centimetre high wooden 'dolly' is set up on a dog-legged metal pole and players, usually divided into two teams of six, throw sticks at the dolly trying to knock it off without hitting the pole.

Not far from the church in Oxford where I was based, a local pub called The Folly Bridge Inn (now renamed The White House) boasted its own Aunt Sally pitch in the back yard. Some church members realised that this presented a wonderful opportunity for the church to engage informally with our neighbours and decided to form an Aunt Sally team based at The Folly.

The team would play on a weekly basis from May to September in the local leagues of the Oxford and District Aunt Sally Association which regularly attracted 120 teams with over 1,400 players taking part. Our church team was securely placed in the lower ranks!

Everyone enjoyed the weekly contests whatever the final outcome: very occasionally we covered ourselves in glory but almost invariably we were well beaten. The gatherings resulted in a number of informal conversations about why we had formed a church team to compete in the league, and gradually seeds of faith were sown. Then one night, at 11.03 p.m., when last orders had just been taken and closing time had been called, the key question came – from Paul the landlord as he was drawing a pint.

From the day we had first approached him about forming a team Paul had been intrigued as to why a group from the local church would want to come to the pub to play Aunt Sally. But he had asked few questions, and spent the ensuing weeks quietly observing us and how we engaged with each other and our opponents in victory and defeat. As I leant against the bar Paul casually asked, 'So what's this Christianity all about, then?'

It was the very question the church team had been longing to hear during our evenings in the pub – but not at 11.03 p.m. when weariness was beginning to take its toll and time was limited. Perhaps that's why Paul had chosen this moment to ask the question!

With no time to work out a comprehensive reply, I

found myself saying, 'Well, Paul, imagine if someone had died in your place to save you, would you ever forget him?' His reply left me completely stunned.

'I haven't,' he said.

'What do you mean, you haven't?'

'Didn't you know, before I became a publican I served in the army?' he replied. I'd had no idea.

Paul continued with a most remarkable story. 'I was serving in Northern Ireland. One night six of us were patrolling up and down the streets of Belfast, alternately on foot and in an armoured vehicle. After one foot patrol, I was just about to climb back into the armoured vehicle when one of the guys said he was stronger than me. I challenged him to a wrestle – on the understanding that whoever lifted the other into the vehicle was the stronger. We wrestled and, after a short struggle, he lifted me into the vehicle. We shook hands, I accepted he was stronger than me and we drove off. A few hundred yards down the road there was a fracas in a side street, our vehicle stopped and we opened the door – the guy who had won our little contest had been last in, so he was the first out, just in front of me. The moment he stepped out of the vehicle a shot rang out and he was killed, right in front of me. Instantly I realised he had taken "my" bullet.'

We looked at each other across the bar. 'Could you ever forget him, Paul?' I asked. His reply was predictable and unprintable.

'That, Paul,' I said, 'is one of the reasons we go to

church, to remember the sacrifice Jesus made for us on the Cross but, unlike your friend, that is not the end of the story for Jesus. His resurrection from the dead offers the promise of new life for all who believe and trust in him. That's why we worship him, and that is why we want to share the good news of what he has done for everybody.'

Emil Brunner, a twentieth-century theologian, once memorably stated: 'A church without mission is like a fire without burning.' That night, at 11.03 p.m. in The Folly pub, a spark was ignited which marked the beginning of long, fruitful conversations, first with Paul, and then other members of the community over the ensuing weeks. All this was the result of a simple decision by church members to form an Aunt Sally team and a question asked over the bar late one night.

'Always be prepared to give an answer to everyone who asks you to give a reason for the hope that you have. But do this with gentleness and respect... For Christ also suffered once for sins, the righteous for the unrighteous, to bring you to God. He was put to death in the body but made alive by the Spirit.'

1 Peter 3:15,18

BUDGERIGAR

'I once had a sparrow alight upon my shoulder for a moment while I was hoeing in a village garden, and I felt that I was more distinguished by that circumstance than I should have been by any epaulet I could have worn.'

Henry David Thoreau

The time of local elections was approaching fast, and unexpectedly the local council approached the church to see if we were willing for the church hall to be used as a polling station. This presented an excellent opportunity to draw the local community into the hall and my immediate response was that the church would be delighted to help out.

There was one problem – the elections were to be held on a Thursday. But Thursdays were the one day of the week when the church provided a regular lunch for homeless and marginalised people in the community. It was always a well-supported venture, much valued by those who regularly came along, and I was very aware that if the lunch were to be abandoned for the day to give priority to a polling station, the underprivileged visitors could feel even more marginalised.

After pondering the issue we decided to go ahead with hosting the polling station. If the weather permitted we would put tables up outside the church and feed all comers in the open air. We had never tried this before but thought it might well serve to publicise the lunches. If it were wet we would move the lunch into the church. Problem solved!

Everyone anxiously scanned the forecast as the day approached and in the event it was a dry, sunny day so all could go ahead as planned. Tables for lunch were placed outside the church and the voters used the hall. What followed was a quite remarkable event.

All was going well, a steady stream of voters came to register their votes, and the food was being prepared for lunch in the church hall kitchen. The usual faces turned up for a bite, together with a couple of newcomers, and it was then I saw out of the corner of my eye one of the regulars, Paul, walking down the road towards the church. He looked so very sad, his shoulders slumped and his face looking down towards the pavement.

'What's up, Paul?' I enquired as he drew near. He replied, 'It's my budgerigar, John. Last night he was having his evening exercise flying around my flat but I'd forgotten to close my window. It was only slightly ajar but he spotted it and the last I saw he was flying away over Oxford.'

Paul was completely devastated. He had experienced

a difficult childhood living with adoptive parents in Scotland, and had spent a number of years in youth detention centres and prison. He could barely read or write and only occasionally had found work as a lorry driver. In recent months Paul had been coming along to the church, food being a particularly attractive option, and I had been pondering how best to explain the good news of God's love to him. Within the next thirty minutes a 'sign and wonder' would answer my questions.

'Take a seat, Paul,' I said, 'and you can tell me all about it. I'll go and fetch a plateful of food for you.' I returned and sat down opposite Paul while he told me exactly what had happened the previous evening. For Paul, his budgerigar was his most prized possession, his greatest friend. It was dependent upon him, didn't answer him back or belittle him in any of the ways people usually treated Paul and was, above all, faithful. The budgie was always there (in its cage!) when he got home, and chirped in response to his call.

Alas, in his eagerness to give the bird some exercise, Paul had overlooked that his window was still slightly open and, before he realised what was happening, the budgerigar had made its escape into the night. For many of the hours that followed, Paul wept; he had lost his best friend in the world. So, on that particular Thursday he came to lunch not primarily for the free food, which he always enjoyed, but to share his grief.

As I listened to Paul, I felt a large measure of his sadness – and increasing helplessness. Lone budgerigars are invariably mobbed by birds when they fly in the open air and the chances of this one having survived the night, let alone being recaptured, were very slim.

At that moment, I looked over Paul's shoulder and saw a bird flying in the sky. Nearer and nearer it came until, to my incredulity, it flew down onto the table where I was sitting with Paul. It was HIS budgerigar! Almost overcome with excitement, Paul leant forward and picked the bird up in his hands – to be honest I thought he was going to crush it to death! He kissed it and kissed it. 'My bird!' he said. 'It's come back to me!'

I retrieved a cardboard box from the church hall and Paul gently placed the bird inside and quickly put the lid on the box. We then tied some string around it so Paul could carry his bird back to his flat in the centre of Oxford, about half a mile from the church hall (as the budgerigar flies) across the River Thames and the inner city ring road. He shared a prayer of thanksgiving to God and returned home almost skipping down the road with joy.

The living God revealing his infinite love to those who cannot read or write! How amazing it was for all of us who were there to see how God had acted that lunchtime – using a sign and wonder that communicated God's love to the needy, not merely to Paul but to all of us privileged to be present on that polling day. We had provided the lunch, circumstances created the context, God – only God – provided the sign and wonder.

The following Sunday, Paul was invited to the front

of church to tell the congregation what had happened the previous Thursday. His face was radiant as he nervously retold the unforgettable events of that lunchtime. When he finished, the whole congregation burst out in spontaneous applause – the first time in his life that Paul had been applauded by such a gathering of people. He returned to his seat sure that the personal love of God embraced him securely.

Not only had God taught Paul a lesson, he had taught all of us a profound truth. Truly, '[God] is able to do immeasurably more than all we ask or imagine, according to his power that is at work within us' (Ephesians 3:20).

> 'Are not two sparrows sold for a penny? Yet not one of them will fall to the ground outside your Father's care… So don't be afraid; you are worth more than many sparrows.'
>
> *Matthew 10:29,31*

CHOCOLATE

The botanical name for chocolate is 'Theobroma cacao'. Translated from the Latin, Theobroma means 'God food.'

Whatever one's place in life's grand scheme of things, for many of us chocolate invariably has a place in the day – this is especially true for a former Archbishop of Canterbury. In February 2007, Lord George Carey came to speak at our church parish weekend which was being held at Lee Abbey in North Devon. During the course of the weekend the subject of chocolate came up and it transpired that Lord Carey is a chocoholic of the first order! An idea began to form in my mind...

The following year the parish was planning and preparing, together with all the other churches in Keynsham, near Bristol, a year-long mission in the wider community called 'More to Life'.* Each month of 2008 the mission was going to focus on a different passion in life,

---

* An account and background to the mission can be read in *More to Life: A Model for Mission in the Local Church in the 21st Century*, No. 90, Evangelism Series, Grove Books, Cambridge.

those that engaged our neighbours. Martin Buber, a Jewish theologian, argues that the thinnest veil between mankind and God lies in the realm of our passions, for it is mankind's Creator who has sown this passion into our hearts. He writes, 'If a man lends his will to the direction of his passions, he begins the movement to holiness which God completes.' During the year of More to Life, within each monthly theme, faith issues and biblical perspectives were to be interwoven with various talks and presentations of broad appeal to the wider community. The chosen theme for June 2008, 'Food', was based around such events as picnics, street parties, a 'Ready, Steady, Cook' competition and, of course, chocolate!

Keynsham had long-established links with the chocolate industry. In the 1920s, the Fry's division of the British Cocoa and Chocolate Company (which had been formed following a merger between Fry's and Cadbury's) moved to the Somerdale site in Keynsham where chocolate was manufactured for the next ninety years, until the factory's eventual closure in 2011. Both the Fry and Cadbury families were staunch Quakers who in the nineteenth century, as non-conformists, were not allowed to attend university; only members of the established church were allowed in. Consequently much of the Quakers' energy was devoted to the social reform and transformation of social and industrial society in Victorian Britain, and this had a far-reaching effect upon communities where they established manufacturing. Quaker companies invested in community facilities – including housing, education, health provision and sports facilities, and emphasised the importance of integrity and good relational values among the management and factory workers and in their dealings with customers. These values significantly shaped the town of Keynsham, with many local people employed in the factory and provided with housing and fine social and sports facilities. It is sad to see that many of those foundational values have been lost in the modern corporate world of big business.

Given this strong link between Keynsham and Cadbury's, when the local churches laid plans for the mission in 2008 it seemed a good idea to hold a 'Chocolate Sunday' in the 'Food' month of June. We planned to give out free chocolate and hire an industrial chocolate fountain to use in the local park during an afternoon of fun and games; concluding with an open-air 'Songs of Praise' with hymns and songs chosen by leading members of the community. Knowing his love of chocolate, who better to invite as our speaker than Lord Carey? Surely the offer of a trip round the then still-functioning Cadbury's factory would clinch it? We were not disappointed, and a memorable day was in the offing.

The More to Life mission was building up a good momentum as each month passed and, in particular, one 'happening' reminded us that God was very much part of proceedings. The theme for April was 'Hope', Easter being celebrated in that month, and we were joined for those weeks by a team of students from

Trinity Theological College, Bristol, who made a great contribution to the mission in the community.

Shortly after they had returned to college I received a large envelope through the post containing an A4-sized booklet and a letter from the student leader of the group, Adrian Jones. The letter included the following words: 'When I got back to my house in Bath after the mission, I was sifting through the piles of stuff in my "office" and came across this booklet. I think it might interest you.' Indeed it did! The full-colour booklet, entitled *More to Life*, had been written for the Millennium by the churches in Bath and had been beautifully produced by the Deo Gloria Trust. I read it with increasing delight, for it presented the Christian faith and the life and significance of Jesus so clearly and relevantly. It was an ideal gift for the Millennium and, more to the point, an ideal gift in a year of mission, especially one also entitled (unwittingly!) 'More to Life'!

I immediately rang up Deo Gloria Trust, explained the background to the community-wide More to Life mission, and asked if they had any copies left. 'Funny you should ask,' was the reply, 'we have only just been saying we need to clear our shelves in the warehouse and we have 3,000 of those booklets we want to clear!' 'How much are they?' I asked. The man answering the phone said, 'Seventy-five pence or £1 each, I believe, but they may be cheaper in bulk. I'll ask the boss and let you know.' Within a week I had a call from the company to announce, 'We'll send all 3,000 of the booklets to you at a cost of 10p each, post free.' The deal was struck – immediately. What a gift!

The planned events for June had started well with a Sunday afternoon street party followed by a well-attended 'Ready, Steady, Cook' evening at one of the local schools. As the days passed we began to study the long range forecasts with greater than usual interest, aware that Chocolate Sunday in particular needed a dry day if it was to make the maximum impact. Four days before the appointed Sunday, a large van drew up outside our house and several large boxes were unloaded – the *More to Life* booklets had arrived at the perfect time!

Chocolate Sunday dawned with June sun shining down and although a few heavy scattered showers were forecast, the amplification system, chocolate fountain and various all-age games were set up in the park and the fun began. It was a glorious occasion. The chocolate fountain alone had over 1,400 'hits': no guessing was needed when a young boy from the local primary school came up and said, 'Guess what I've been doing?' His face was plastered with chocolate!

The open air 'Songs of Praise', concluding the afternoon, was a huge success with Lord Carey in fine form, fortified by his tour around the chocolate factory the previous evening. Over 500 copies of the *More to Life* booklet were distributed during the afternoon and many of the wider community of Keynsham enjoyed the activities, the singing, Lord Carey's address – and the free bars of Fair Trade chocolate on offer!

As the sun set that evening I reflected, together with a number of others involved with the planning of the year-long mission, on how so many things had come together over a span of many months to create such a memorable day – the discovery and availability of a notable 'chocoholic', the unearthing of the *More to Life* booklet in Adrian's study, Deo Gloria's generosity, the timely arrival of the books, the fine weather (despite very heavy showers just a couple of miles away) to name just a few. Once again we had been reminded that 'in him all things hold together' (Colossians 1:17), even chocolate!

'Taste and see that the Lord is good.'

Psalm 34:8

DAD

'Our brightest blazes are often caused by unexpected sparks.'

Samuel Johnson

The kids were both asleep, the cats curled up on the sofa and the house was quiet. The phone rang and it was my father, who had recently been having a few health issues. He wanted to let us know the outcome of a recent visit to the doctor.

Fifteen years earlier he had had a heart valve replaced and, apparently, his heartbeat had now become rather irregular. Dad went on to tell us that the doctor had explained the problem could be corrected in hospital by the administration of an electric shock and that the date for the hospital appointment had been fixed. We were grateful to know the outcome of the visit to the doctor, promised to pray for him, and said we looked forward to seeing him shortly when he was due to visit us for a weekend.

A few days later, as we were praying for him, both Chris and I had a strong sense that when the 'pre-med' was administered, before the anaesthetic and subsequent procedure, Dad should simply say in his heart, 'Jesus is Lord'. He had been a regular churchgoer all his life, was a God-fearing man, but had no personal experience of a relationship with God. He had witnessed the events surrounding Mum's illness and death (see *Lying in Bed*) two years earlier, did not question the reality of Mum's experience but appeared to have been 'looking in from the outside' as events unfolded. All this was about to change.

Dad duly paid his visit to us a few days before going into hospital, yet somehow the right opportunity to share what Chris and I 'knew' we had to say to him did not present itself. He climbed into our car for me to take him back to the station in Bristol and as we drove down the road, just minutes from the station, the moment suddenly seemed right. Somewhat defensively, not wanting to appear too insistent, I said, 'Dad, when Chris and I were praying for you earlier this week, we both sensed we had to tell you something. In the past, whenever you've had an operation, you've said that when the pre-med is administered you quietly pray, "Into thy hand I commit my spirit." This time Chris and I believe that in your heart you should you should simply declare, "Jesus is Lord".'

I need not have worried about Dad's reaction; he just said, 'Yes, of course I will, John. Thank you both so much for praying for me.' What I didn't say was that in truth the hardest thing had been finding the right time

17

to pass the suggestion on to him. On my return home, Chris was delighted to hear news of the conversation.

The day of the hospital appointment dawned. Through the day our thoughts and prayers were constantly with Dad as we went about our business, wondering how the procedure was going, whether he would have to stay in overnight and, in particular, whether he would be able to get the last train back to Princes Risborough from Paddington before a 24-hour train strike that was due to commence that evening. Our phone rang just before 9.00 p.m. and it was Dad, ringing from home! As he recounted the events of the day, we listened with an increasing sense of incredulity and wonder.

Dad had arrived at St Thomas' Hospital, London, in good time (he was a firm time-keeper) and, at the appointed hour, had a series of heart checks in order to ascertain precisely what the medics needed to do in theatre. Shortly afterwards, in went the 'pre-med', up went his prayer and, following the anaesthetic, he was wheeled into the theatre. The next thing he remembered was lying in a bed in the ward, looking up at the nurse, and asking, 'How did it all go? Have you fixed it?' The nurse replied that when Dad got into the theatre, some final checks showed his heart was beating regularly and no electric shock was needed. So he had simply been wheeled out and given time to 'wake up' from his anaesthetic. He was free to leave when he felt he had fully recovered.

After lying there a short while gathering his thoughts, Dad got out of bed and began to get dressed. As he did so he found himself 'talking' to God in a way he had never done before – in a conversational manner, sensing God's presence right beside him. Having thanked the nursing staff, Dad left the hospital and summoned a taxi. It was just before 6.30 p.m., and the last train from Paddington to Princes Risborough was due to leave at 7.00 p.m., leaving plenty of time for a journey of normally less than fifteen minutes. However, that night there were a number of road works and the taxi driver seemed very unsure of how to avoid the congestion. The clock was ticking – 6.50 p.m., 6.54 p.m., 6.58 p.m... Sitting in the back of the taxi, Dad found himself completely unfazed by this turn of events and prayed silently, 'Well, Lord, if you want me to spend a night in London, that's what I'll do.' Not once did he find himself getting irritated with the taxi driver which, given his careful time-keeping, surprised him.

It was 7.03 p.m. when they arrived at Paddington, and Dad was resigned to a night in London. However, when he entered the station and looked at the departures board he saw that the train to Princes Risborough had been delayed and would not be leaving until 7.15 p.m. What a delight!

When Dad finally arrived home he immediately picked the phone up. 'You'll never guess what has happened today,' he told me rather breathlessly, and proceeded to recount the day's events. He finished with the statement, 'It is just amazing! Why haven't you told me about all this before?' We both burst out laughing.

Quite simply, Dad was never the same again. He lived for five more years and during that time he read the Bible from cover to cover – using a Selwyn Hughes' *Bible in a Year* guide – and had an appetite for God's Word that never left him. His prayer life was revitalised and he truly was alive in the Spirit. He had always been a faithful, respected figure in business and the local community, and his two passions in life were gardening and bird watching. Having met with God in such a personal way at 71 years of age, these passions and his character were imbued with a new life that was apparent to all.

His one regret? 'John, why didn't I discover this as a young man?' This was not a question I could answer, but I was profoundly grateful for God's patience and persistence – and Dad's openness to God's love.

'If you declare with your mouth, "Jesus is Lord," and believe in your heart that God raised him from the dead, you will be saved.'

Romans 10:9

ESCAPE

'It is easy to take freedom for granted, when you have never had it taken from you.'

Author unknown

It was a gloriously sunny late autumn Friday morning – at last! Fridays were our day off in the parish and Chris and I decided to go for a walk in the Chilterns, through one of our favourite valleys near Christmas Common. We parked the car, put on our boots and strolled along a delightful path with beams of sunlight coming through the tall beech trees overhead, each adorned with the most stunning array of yellow, gold and fiery orange leaves.

Suddenly we both heard an unusual rustling noise and stopped. A short way ahead there seemed to be movement in the light undergrowth to the right of the path. We moved forward slowly and quietly, not wanting to disturb anything but curious to know more. We had not gone more than fifty yards before we saw the reason for the unexpected sound – a large stag with huge antlers had somehow got caught up in a camouflage net which had been tied to a tree.

Chris and I looked on with a mixture of horror and helplessness. Neither of us was carrying a mobile phone so we couldn't easily summon help, and we were both aware of the size of the animal. As we stood there and studied the scene, it became clear the deer had been trapped for some time. Entwined around the antlers, the net had worn a groove into the soft velvety outer bone as the animal had struggled to get free, and clearly exhaustion was beginning to set in. There was a rather wild-eyed look about the creature, not immediately helped by the sudden appearance on the scene of two unexpected walkers.

We both stood stock still for some minutes and wondered what we could do. Eventually I turned to Chris and said, 'I'm going to see if we can set it free. We'll have to go very slowly; this could take some time.'

We decided (Chris with some reluctance) that the best idea was for her to stand still, and pray, while I very slowly edged towards the animal with the aim of reaching the end of the net attached to a tree. This took several minutes but eventually I got there, the animal tugging more furiously at the net during my approach. Having reached the tree and putting my hand on the net, I stood still, remained completely silent and steadily looked the creature in the eye.

For some minutes, neither the creature nor I moved as we looked at each other. Inch by inch, I then began to move closer. He returned my gaze and was taut as a coiled spring; every moment I wondered if he was going to leap towards me. I quietly began to speak to the deer, still looking him in the eye, explaining what we wanted to do (even though the animal could not have understood!) and trying to make reassuring noises.

Eventually I reached a point where I could take hold of one of the antlers; I was now close enough to realise not only how deeply the net had worn a groove into the bone but also how dry the nose of the animal was. Clearly it must have been trapped for some time and was very thirsty. As I held the antler I grasped the net in my other hand and managed to untangle it, at which point the deer, almost triumphantly, leapt up and literally bounded off into the wood. We never saw the creature again.

Almost motionless, Chris and I looked at each other, reflecting on what we had just witnessed – the struggling animal entwined in the net; our horror at the sight and deep desire to set the creature free; its initial fear as it saw us, and the redoubling of its efforts to escape, not only from the net but from us; the time, patience and persistence the whole 'rescue operation' took; the deer's amazing sense of delight as it bounded away free from its entrapment; our thrill and joy at seeing freedom bestowed on such a fine creature. For both of us it was a truly memorable event.

Many years later, this episode was vividly brought back to my mind early one morning in the days leading up to Easter in 2008. Every Monday and Wednesday I habitually went for an early morning run around a nearby sports field that bordered fields where sheep grazed. This week, on the Monday, I had noticed a sheep standing on its own near one of the water troughs close to a barbed wire fence. I thought nothing of it until, on the Wednesday, I spotted the same sheep in exactly the same place, still on its own, far from the others.

Intrigued, I climbed over the wooden fence and approached the sheep. I soon realised that its thick woollen coat had got caught up in the barbed wire, securely trapping the animal. By now it was very weak and barely able to stand, struggling unsuccessfully to get away as I drew near. All the while making calming noises, I was able to get hold of the barbed wire and gradually tug it away from the sheep's coat. After a few minutes, the sheep, exhausted and seriously dehydrated, slowly gathered itself and managed to get to the trough and have a drink. I collected some loose hay that had been scattered nearby by the farmer, piled it near the sheep so there was some food readily accessible, and returned to my run, reflecting on all that had just happened.

Being the middle of Holy Week, the events only served to remind me of the truth that lies at the heart of the gospel, a truth that in my early years I had struggled against and run away from – for more than thirty years. Like the deer and the sheep, I ran away from the One who wanted to save me, to set me free; from the One who was so patient and persevering with me; from the One who said, 'I have come that you may have life and have it to the full.' How could I have been so foolish?

There are many reasons, of course. Although I had been brought up to go to church, I had never 'heard' the gospel clearly explained and gradually the habit of attending services declined. I discovered I had 'other things to do' – certainly my obsession for sport filled my time and, over the years, increasingly I became absorbed in my studies, teaching and, after getting married, helping to look after a growing family. Days and weeks seemingly flew by, life was fulfilling and challenging and there seemed little time for much else. If I'm honest, there was also a nagging suspicion that if I turned to God I would have to reorder my priorities and a fear that maybe my passions in life would have to be sidelined.

And yet the 'God question' did not go away. Like the deer and sheep, I too had become 'caught up and entangled' in my journey through life and it was only after a period of wrestling and struggling that, by the grace of God, I was set free. Only then did I begin to taste the true wonder of life in all its fullness – a life that embraced the passions on my heart but put them into the context of God's love.

How foolish I had been to resist for all those years!

> Jesus said: 'Very truly I tell you, everyone who sins is a slave to sin. Now a slave has no permanent place in the family, but a son belongs to it for ever. So if the Son sets you free, you will be free indeed.'
>
> John 8: 34–36

FA CUP
QUARTER-FINAL
1980

'When I pray, coincidences happen; when I don't, they don't.'

Archbishop William Temple

'Watford will play Arsenal.' It may be difficult to imagine the degree of excitement these words generated inside the head of a 35-year-old geography teacher and father of two. However, when I heard the announcement of the FA Cup quarter-final draw in February 1980 my heart leapt and I exclaimed, 'Yes!' As it turned out, I was about to learn a significant lesson from God.

I have been an avid supporter of Watford Football Club since the day my father took me to see them play Aldershot Town FC in 1954. Living in Pinner in north-west London, Watford FC was my nearest football league club and it was with great anticipation that I attended a match at Vicarage Road for the first time.

Watford won the match 6–1 and, not surprisingly, I was hooked from that moment. Dad and I soon became season ticket holders and, as I rushed home each Friday afternoon at the end of another week at school, I eagerly anticipated turning to the back pages of the weekly local paper offering all the latest club news. In subsequent decades, wherever I moved to, including Nigeria, redirecting the postal delivery of the *Watford Observer* was one of my first priorities, thus keeping me in touch with events at the Club.

As you might imagine, this passion for an unfashionable club was seldom fully appreciated by the rest of the family and my friends, although there was one moment when Chris and the children had good reason to be thankful. One Saturday afternoon in the mid 1970s, we were travelling by car from Kano to Jos in northern Nigeria, listening to the football on BBC World Service. Radio reception was not very reliable, so when the time for the full time scores approached we pulled off the road and waited for the results to be announced. Watford were playing in the Third Division at the time and had a home match, so we had to wait a little while.

Having heard the result we pulled back onto the road to resume our journey, only to be confronted a few minutes later by a scene of complete carnage. A 'mammy wagon' overloaded with passengers had overtaken us while we were parked on the roadside and shortly after had collided with a large lorry. The roads in Nigeria were pitted with potholes and accidents were frequent, but seldom had we seen such a chaotic, bloody scene. Bodies were scattered widely and several other vehicles had been damaged. At once Chris and I looked at each other, thinking: 'If we hadn't pulled over to hear the results, and hadn't waited so long for Watford's result to be read out, we might well have been involved in the accident ourselves.' One of the fans' popular chants on the terraces was 'Watford till I die'; we so nearly did that afternoon…

News of the 1980 FA Cup quarter-final draw came through a few years later when we were back in the UK and living in High Wycombe. However, my elation at the prospect of welcoming one of the 'big' clubs to Vicarage Road was soon to be significantly dampened. I discovered the sale of tickets for the match had been arranged to be held at 10 a.m. on a Sunday morning at the Club offices. Normally that would not have been a problem, after all there had been previous occasions when I had slept overnight on the pavement outside the ground to ensure a successful purchase, but on this particular Sunday I faced an acute dilemma. My vicar had asked me to lead the prayers at the morning service and I had a choice to make: fulfil my commitment to lead prayers or travel to buy tickets for one of the biggest matches (at that time) in Watford's history. Which was it to be?

I agonised long and hard (honestly!), praying for wisdom and resolve to make the right decision. Yes, I could have arranged for someone else to lead prayers that morning, but what was that saying about my commitment to God? What were my priorities? I had not long been a Christian and I was keenly aware of the importance of seeking to honour God in the multitude of daily choices that we make.

A whole series of calculations began to revolve around my mind. The service began at 10.00 a.m., the prayers would be over some time before 11.00 a.m., I could stay for communion and then nip out of the service before the end. The journey time from High Wycombe to Watford on a Sunday morning was about 45 minutes and I could perhaps be at the ground before midday. However, with people having been queuing from the early hours, would there still be tickets available?

After weighing up all the options I decided I would lead the prayers, leave as quickly as I could, and drive to Watford more in hope than expectation. In the event the service went on longer than I had anticipated, I stayed until the end and finally got away from church little before 11.30 a.m. I wondered whether it was still worth making the journey but ignored my doubts and drove as quickly as I could, fully anticipating that my expedition would end in failure. I arrived at the ground with no one in sight. The queue for tickets had obviously dispersed and I drove down to the main gates with a sinking heart, pulling up just as the man on duty was pushing the gates together to lock them up. I wound down the car window and said, somewhat breathlessly, 'I've just come up from High Wycombe, I couldn't leave any earlier, is it possible to still get a ticket?'

To my surprise (and delight) the man held the gate open, told me to park the car, and directed me under the main stand. I walked down a corridor and into a room where about six fellows sat around a long table, bagging up huge piles of money. They turned around defensively as I approached and tentatively enquired if there was any possibility of getting a ticket, explaining I had only just managed to get there from High Wycombe. To my incredulity one of the men simply asked, 'How many do you want?'

How many did I want?! That was the last question I had anticipated being asked, as there had been a limit of two tickets per supporter in the queue and I was sure the demand that morning would have far exceeded supply. In my innocence I didn't realise that when the 'Sold Out' sign went up there were always some tickets held back for various reasons. So I did a quick mental calculation, thinking of colleagues I worked with who had come to Watford before, and replied, 'Well, if it's possible I would like five.' Without hesitation the man picked up a number of tickets from the table. 'One, two, three, four, five,' he counted, and then handed them over. I could barely contain my glee as I wrote out a cheque for the necessary amount. The fellow on the gate smiled as I walked back to the car with a spring in

30

my step, 'Glad your journey wasn't a wasted one,' he said. So was I!

As I drove back from the Vicarage Road stadium, amazed at the turn of events, I suddenly found myself breaking out into song as the words of a popular chorus we sang in church came into my mind. 'Seek ye first the kingdom of God and his righteousness, and all these things will be added unto you, Allelu, alleluia!' These words are based on those of Jesus when he presented arguably the most magnificent sermon ever delivered, the Sermon on the Mount (Matthew 5–7); as I sang out the song that Sunday lunchtime, it was as if Jesus was speaking the words to me at that moment, with a smile in his eyes.

The course of events that day taught me a significant lesson. Yes, choices do have to be made, and the Christian pilgrimage repeatedly requires us to make them. For example, what does it mean to put God first in our daily living? What priority should our passions (those various activities that consume much of our time and resources) have in the ordering of our days? How can we engage with God in the midst of our passions? In each and every instance there is a signpost to the answer in God's Word – the Bible. As the psalmist so aptly writes: 'Your word is a lamp to my feet and a light for my path' (Psalm 119:105). God's word includes both guidelines for living and also wonderful promises, and both are designed to lead us to life in all its fullness.

What did it mean for me to 'seek first the kingdom

of God' when confronted with the dilemma of what to do that Sunday morning? In retrospect it may seem a very straightforward decision, yet my deep passion for a football club was in collision with a commitment I had made to serve God.

In making the choice I did, the subsequent offer of five tickets ('Immeasurably more than I could have asked or even imagined' Ephesians 3:20) provided me with an unforgettable lesson: Put God first, digest his Word, trust in him, await the outcome of his promises… and be prepared for a surprise!

> Jesus said: 'Seek first his kingdom and his righteousness, and all these things will be given to you.'
>
> *Matthew 6:33*

GEOGRAPHY

'If Jesus returned tomorrow, he'd be a geographer.'

Professor James M. Houston

It was a sunny summer lunchtime in 1990 and I was sitting at a table in the garden of The Perch, a quiet riverside pub in Oxford. The conversation took an unexpected turn. 'You do know, John, don't you, that if Jesus returned tomorrow he'd be a geographer!' said my companion. I laughed! Having studied geography at university and then taught it for fifteen years, I was intrigued at the suggestion. 'Tell me more, Jim.' Sitting opposite me clasping his beer was Jim Houston, an erstwhile geography don at Oxford University who at the time was Professor of Spiritual Theology at Regent College in Vancouver, Canada.

I had first bumped into Jim in London in 1985, at a conference I was attending to hear Revd Dr John Stott, Rector Emeritus of All Souls, Langham Place, deliver a series of lectures on the first three chapters of Genesis in the Bible. To fill my spare hours at the conference, I decided to book into a lecture Jim was delivering entitled 'A Spirituality for the 20th Century'; it was a compelling hour and I have continued to feed on its content until the present day.

Some years later I discovered Jim was coming to Oxford, where I was then living. He was visiting at the invitation of the C.S. Lewis Institute, which organises an annual summer lecture programme and, recalling how inspirational I had found him before, I decided to attend another of his lectures. It, too, proved compelling and at its conclusion I asked Jim whether he'd have time to share lunch at a local pub. So it was that we came to be at The Perch.

'Well, John,' Jim continued, warming to his theme of Jesus as a geographer, 'no one would dispute that the world, notwithstanding its beauty, is full of brokenness – environmentally, relationally, economically and financially. Yet, consider for a moment the list of Nobel Prize winners over recent years – each one is an analyst. The world is full of analysts, "experts who know more and more about less and less", and consequently so many decisions are made that lack a coherent vision. Whether in the realm of politics, the economy, education, health care or whatever, what the world desperately requires – locally, nationally and globally – is synthesists, "people who can examine and respond to issues from a much wider perspective, from all angles". In short we need, above all, people who can bring coherence to this broken world.'

Jim reflected on his former role in the Oxford University geography department and continued, 'Geography is the supreme synthesising subject – embracing the whole of the created order, both physical and human. Surely, it is only logical to argue that Jesus would be a geographer, because the Bible informs us: "in him all things hold together… God was pleased to have all his fullness dwell in him, and through him to reconcile… all things" (Colossians 1:17,19,20).' He paused and we both smiled.

It was for me, a geographer by training, an engaging argument and my mind went back some twenty-five years to when I was halfway through my geography degree. One afternoon, in the midst of a lecture on the evolution of landforms, I had experienced an 'epiphany moment' when it suddenly dawned upon me that the subject I was studying had a far deeper significance than I had ever realised, a significance that was not merely 'informational' but essentially relational in nature. That is to say, geography is not merely about the study of places but ultimately about the quest for a greater understanding of that which brings coherence to the whole created order.

Truth to tell, I had made the decision to study geography at university because I believed that it would allow me time to devote most of my energy to pursuing my main passion in life, sport – particularly rugby and cricket. Yes, I was interested in the subject but in a superficial way, primarily seeing it as a means to an end.

From that moment in the midst of a geomorphology lecture, my perspective on the subject shifted; sport certainly remained a passion (it still does) but it was now accompanied by a new-found passion for geography.

As I continued as an undergraduate I became pre-occupied with a persistent and worryingly nagging question. When I graduated, what was I going to do? I considered various options, including research, banking, and entering my father's insurance business, but remained undecided... that is, until I heard about Voluntary Service Overseas. VSO had been established a few years earlier, in 1958, and offered the opportunity for graduates to work overseas in the 'developing world' for one or two years. As a graduate in geography, the only 'expertise' I could offer would be as a teacher, and I reasoned that this would enable me to continue pursuing the two main passions in my life while affording time and space for me to think about what path I wanted to take in life. I felt sure that a year overseas, removed from 'distractions' of family, friends and the familiar, would be a timely move. I had little idea how true this would prove to be.

Having made my application to VSO, I was delighted to discover I had been accepted. I was offered the opportunity to teach in a secondary school in a remote area of north-western Nigeria, not far from the borders of the Sahara desert. Within two months of my graduation I boarded a plane to fly out. (See *Nigeria*.)

Upon arrival, one of the first things I came to realise (for this was well before the days of the Internet – indeed, the telephone was a rarity where I was living) was how precious the delivery of mail from the UK became. The post was delivered once a week and it was with a keen sense of anticipation that I made the trek to the post office, to look in my personal mailbag, to see if any letters had arrived.

On one occasion I was delighted to discover a small package from my sister, Angela, containing a couple of books by Pierre Teilhard de Chardin, a French philosopher, palaeontologist and Jesuit priest. If I'm honest, back in the UK I would never have given myself time to read the books (too many distractions) but out in Nigeria it proved a timely gift and an engaging read, addressing many of the questions that had been swirling around in my mind for some time. In *The Phenomenon of Man,* de Chardin presents a sweeping cosmic, coherent vision of the origins and evolution of life in all its variety, embracing natural, human and scientific realms. Given my passion for geography and the associated quest for relational well being, I found de Chardin's argument deeply engaging and was further intrigued by the way he reconciled scientific enquiry and spiritual faith, thus helping to break down the 'sacred and secular divide' that impoverishes so much of our thinking in the western world.

As the year in Nigeria continued, I sensed a

profound change beginning to take place in my perspective on life. In retrospect I recognise it was a deep awakening of my spiritual journey, a journey that would several years later bring me to faith in Jesus Christ. Having just returned from one of his travels, de Chardin summarised in a single sentence what I was experiencing: 'The journey was over, and I felt keenly how little, of itself, mere displacement in space adds to a man. On returning to his point of departure, unless he has developed his inner life... he is still exactly like everyone else' (*Letters from a Traveller*, 1923).

From the moment I opened that mailbag to discover de Chardin's books, it was not until twenty years later that I found myself sitting down for lunch with Jim Houston at The Perch in Oxford. His comment that Jesus would surely be a geographer, coupled with the laughter and explanation that ensued, was reminiscent of that magical Rubik's Cube moment of triumph when, with one click, everything falls into place! In an instant, hitherto disparate elements in my life – including my passions, the big questions of life, insights of Teilhard de Chardin, the experiences of Africa – all connected.

In that 'epiphany moment' I realised the potential of deep connections embracing all spheres of life – material, relational and spiritual. It was a taste of life in all its fullness, a realisation that truly 'all things hold together in him'.

Never had a pub lunch tasted better!

'He is before all things, and in him all things hold together.'

Colossians 1:17

HASTINGS: COUNTY CRICKET MATCH

The final county cricket match to be played at Hastings before the ground was sold to developers saw a contest between Sussex and Lancashire. The second day of the three-day match was on 29 June 1985. Cricket is one of my passions and when I arrived to serve my curacy in Patcham, near Brighton, I was delighted to discover that two Sussex players, John Spencer and John Barclay (the county captain) lived in the parish and had links with the church. Before long I met up with them and in due course John Barclay invited me to take up the role of chaplain at the county ground in Hove. It was an invitation I was delighted to receive, offering a new sphere of ministry in the world of sport, a world that occupied not a small part of my mind.

When he returned from Hastings, I met up with John Barclay to find out how the match had gone. As he reflected on the game, the cricketer recounted a remarkable episode that had happened on the second day's play, an episode that served to remind him that God's word is 'living and active'.

Sussex were batting in their second innings and building up a commanding lead over Lancashire, with the partnership between opening batsmen, Mendis and Green, already scoring more than 150 runs. It was a pleasant summer late afternoon and Barclay decided to stretch his legs and take a stroll around the boundary to watch the game from different vantage points.

At one point, as he paused to watch the bowler begin the next over, an elderly gentleman sitting on a deckchair nearby turned and asked, 'What's your name and what do you do?' Barclay smiled and said, 'I'm John Barclay, I mainly bowl but I also bat a bit.' In reply the man grunted and in a rather clipped tone replied, 'Ecclesiastes 9:10. Don't forget it,' at which point the man stood up, folded his deckchair and pottered off.

Smiling to himself, John reflected he'd heard many comments in a lifetime spent sauntering around cricket boundaries but never 'Ecclesiastes 9:10'! Somewhat perplexed he returned (rather more purposefully) to the pavilion to retrieve the Bible he always carried in his kit bag. Turning to the verse in Ecclesiastes he read,

'Whatever your hand finds to do, do it with all your might, for in the grave, where you are going, there is neither working nor planning nor knowledge nor wisdom.'

As the cricket meandered on, with Sussex having reached 193–0 by the close of play, John pondered those words. It was clear to him that if Sussex now declared their second innings closed, Lancashire would be faced with the daunting, but not impossible, challenge of scoring 331 runs for victory on the final day, while Sussex had a whole day to bowl Lancashire out for victory. An ideal contest, thought John, who promptly decided to declare and throw down the challenge.

The following day, after about an hour's play, Lancashire were showing no appetite for chasing victory and Sussex's opening bowling attack had made little impact on the batsman. The match was in real danger of petering out into a dull draw. Then suddenly in the midst of an over, as John caught the ball from the wicket keeper to return it to the bowler, those words from Ecclesiastes echoed in his head, 'Whatever your hand finds to do…' 'Perhaps', thought John, 'it's time to bring myself on for a bowl,' and shortly afterwards, having ignored his ever-present self doubts, he took the plunge.

As he walked back to his bowling mark to begin, John looked down at the ball grasped in his hands and repeated to himself, '"Whatever your hands find to do, do it with all your might." Well, Lord, you've given me this gift of bowling; help me to use it to the best of my ability for you.' He turned to bowl his first ball.

Lancashire's second innings ended in the afternoon with a total of 257 runs and Sussex won the match by 73 runs. John Barclay ended up bowling 30 overs (one of the longest spells in his career!) and finished with the figures of 5 wickets for 99 runs. According to his cynical teammates it was the first time he had taken 5 wickets in an innings in living memory (in fact it was three years)!

John returned to our parish with a fresh sense of wonder. Not for a moment was he attributing any magical powers to the words of Scripture, as if all he had to do was open his Bible, read the right verse and, hey presto, all would be well. In fact, by nature full of self-doubts, for many years John had somewhat ruefully reflected that Jesus' words 'They neither toil nor spin' (Matthew 6:28) were a rather more apt comment on his bowling! Rather, John sensed in that unlikely encounter on the boundary in Hastings, while going about his daily task, he had been reminded in extraordinary circumstances that God's word really is living and active (Hebrews 4:12) and is relevant in all spheres of life, not least in his particular passion. He recognised that if we seek to align the way we live our lives with the guidelines we discover in the Bible, we will take progressive steps towards a whole new dimension of life… 'Life in all its fullness.'

Little wonder that the lessons from that encounter on the boundary in Hastings in 1985 remain in John's heart to this day.

> 'Whatever your hand finds to do, do it with all your might.'
>
> *Ecclesiastes 9:10*

IMAGINATION

> 'Imagination is more important than knowledge.'
> *Albert Einstein*
>
> 'People who lean on logic and philosophy and rational exposition end by starving the best part of the mind.'
> *William Butler Yeats*

Imagination requires time and space, increasingly scarce commodities in our time-pressed lives in western society. Much of our life can so easily be caught up in the superficial – our reading (contenting ourselves with headlines and having little interest in explanations), our relationships (speed dating, the exponential rise of electronic communication at the expense of face-to-face encounters) and our busy routines – that we find little room to indulge our imagination. We find ourselves merely existing rather than living.

That is why I believe children are such a gift – and a threat! They are a gift because they are 'at home' in the world of imagination and this can serve to awaken our own. They are a threat because entering into their world, playing and establishing deep relationships with them, requires us to forsake the helter-skelter world of adulthood. Quite simply, children profoundly challenge our priorities!

This was something Jesus demonstrated when the disciples came and asked him: "'Who is greatest in the kingdom of heaven?" [Jesus] called a little child and had him stand among them. And he said, "I tell you the truth, unless you change and become like little children, you will never enter the kingdom of heaven. Therefore, whoever humbles himself like this child is the greatest in the kingdom of heaven. And whoever welcomes a little child like this in my name welcomes me."' (Matthew 18:3–5).

Whenever Jesus uses the phrase 'I tell you the truth' he is about to make an important statement. Here he is underlining the importance of recognising the inherent gifts in a child. Jesus is not saying the kingdom of heaven belongs only to little children – he frequently made it clear that everyone is invited in. Rather, by including children in this way he is showing that the way into the kingdom is not merely by rational means but also requires the exercise of imagination.

Children invariably love hearing stories and indulging their imagination. It is clear from the gospels that Jesus used so many 'stories' and illustrations from everyday life to illuminate his teaching (to young and old alike) because they are invaluable in rekindling our imagination, enabling us to see things differently.

When I became a Christian in the midst of my teaching career, I recognised the significant part that faithful, relevant preaching and teaching had played, and continues to play, in my spiritual journey. A few years later, at the outset of full-time ministry as a curate, the instruction of Paul to his young pastor, Timothy, namely: 'Preach the Word; be prepared in season and out of season; correct, rebuke and encourage – with great patience and careful instruction' (2 Timothy 4:2), served to reinforce this weight of responsibility.

Jesus demonstrates that to 'preach the Word' means more than mere explanation. To be effective, preaching needs to illustrate how the truth of the scriptures and the lessons they provide are connected with every sphere of the living of our daily lives. It is because of this that I am so deeply grateful to God for one particular encounter when I was a curate. That encounter has stayed with me for the rest of my life and taught me a very important lesson.

It was early on a Monday morning and I was walking along the road to meet my training vicar, David, for our weekly team meeting. Suddenly, walking towards me in the distance, I saw a man who had very recently started coming to church. Instinctively, I realised that if I could address him by name it would be a significant gesture – he would know that although he was a newcomer to the church he wasn't merely 'one of a crowd'; rather, he was known by name, he 'counted'. I just 'knew' this could draw him closer to God.

Somewhere in my diary I had the man's name – the problem was, where? I rapidly began to thumb through its pages and as the distance between us became shorter and shorter I still had not found his name. (Personal reminder: John, organise your diary better.) Then, just as I had to look up to acknowledge him I saw his name! 'Morning, Peter,' I said, smiling, 'do hope you have a good week.' 'Thanks, John,' he replied, 'good to see you.' Immediately we had passed each other I 'heard' God say, 'John, if you trust me, I will give you illustrations when you need them. Simply keep your eyes open, moment by moment.'

Rather than trying to store away a complex filing system of illustrations to be retrieved at a future date for use in sermons and talks, I was to trust God to provide examples from the daily round of life. In short I was constantly to exercise my imagination, looking for the hand of God in every circumstance of life. In so doing, the realities of the kingdom of God would be revealed in everyday situations. By the grace of God, that promise has been fulfilled over the subsequent years of my ministry.

It is clear from the gospels that Jesus recognised that illustrations, familiar in the day-to-day experiences of his hearers, had a vital place to play in sharing the living, loving presence of a holy God in the midst of the 'stuff of life'. It is no different today. Each day, whatever it holds, is full of encounters and experiences which, with the help of the imagination, serve to shed light on the

Word of God and his living presence in this world. The appropriate use of these illustrations offers precious food for those who are hungry to know more about the existence and truth of the living God.

'…The basic reality of God is plain enough. Open your eyes and there it is! By taking a long and thoughtful look at what God has created, people have always been able to see what their eyes as such cannot see: eternal power, for instance, and the mystery of his divine being'

Romans 1:20, The Message

JESUS HAS 'JUMPED'

'The only way to make sense out of change is to plunge into it, move with it and join the dance.'

Alan Watts

'Creativity consists largely of rearranging what we know in order to find out what we do not know. Hence, to think creatively, we must be able to look afresh at what we normally take for granted.'

George Kneller

By now you've probably noticed that this book is arranged in alphabetical order, and you may have opened this page looking for something beginning with J. Perhaps you were looking for Jesus? Well, I've used the author's prerogative to move that entry to the end of the book. You'll find out why in due course. There's no need to rush there. Why not read some other stories first?

KERBSIDE ENCOUNTERS

'In everyone's life, at some time, our inner fire goes out. It is then burst into flame by an encounter with another human being. We should all be thankful for those people who rekindle the inner spirit.'

Albert Schweitzer

January 6, 1989, Feast of the Epiphany: 2.45 p.m. on an autumn Saturday afternoon in Marlborough Road, Oxford.

I was seldom seen outside in the parish early on a Saturday afternoon when Watford Football club, the team I ardently support, were shortly to kick off, and it was important for me to have the local radio carefully tuned in for the team news and ensuing commentary. However, on this particular day I had a pastoral visit to make and after lunch I calculated I had just enough time to conclude the visit in an unhurried way and be back in time for the match.

All was going to plan, the pastoral visit had been successfully negotiated and I was pedalling hard on my bike down Marlborough Road, returning to the vicarage and looking forward to kick off. Then I saw a couple with their three young children looking up at the church notice board. I could of course have put my head down and just cycled past – a great temptation as there were only fifteen minutes to the start of the match. Instead, I screeched to a halt at the kerb and smiled. 'I can give them all the information they want in a couple of minutes,' I thought, 'and still be back in time for the match.'

I am eternally grateful that a sense of conviction overcame my natural urge to pass by. In the course of the next ten minutes (I only just missed kick off!) a friendship was begun that has endured to this day. Indeed, I received the following email almost twenty-three years later (before this book was begun):

Indeed it was a providence that we met in such a happenstance way in 1989... we'll never get over that!! It was so ordinarily supernatural if you know what I mean. We were the somewhat lost people from could-have-been-anywhere and you were the vicar on your home turf en route to a regular weekly enjoyment. AND that's GOD!!
Charles

It transpired that the Nienkirchen family had just arrived in Oxford to begin a six-month stay in the city.

Charles Nienkirchen, a professor of Church History at Ambrose University in Calgary, was embarking upon a study leave based at Oxford University, during which time he was going to spend time reflecting upon and writing about prayer. As we talked, Charles looked over my shoulder and saw carved into the stonework of St Matthew's Church the words: 'Lord, teach us to pray.' At that time that entrance was seldom used, as folk entered the church through another door, and the stonework looked rather tired. For Charles, however, it was a 'sign' that perhaps the Lord was calling his family to make St Matthew's their base for the duration of the following months. As we chatted (briefly, you understand, kick off was drawing ever nearer!), I shared the details of the following day's services, we said a short prayer together on the pavement and then parted. I certainly felt there was unfinished business to deal with and very much hoped to see the family the following day. I did, and the rest, as they say, is history!

Neither the Nienkirchens nor I doubt for one moment that the Lord had orchestrated that encounter. In the days and weeks that followed, the Nienkirchen family threw themselves into the life of the church, while Charles spent his days reading and writing about prayer. The fact that we 'happened' to find ourselves bumping into each other on the pavement arose from our being about our daily business, not dissimilar to the way Ruth 'happened' to be in the same field as Boaz when she was gleaning leftover grain in the barley harvest in Bethlehem (Ruth 1:19 – 2:23). For Ruth the consequences of that 'chance' encounter were very far-reaching, eventually placing her in the genealogy of Jesus (Matthew 1:5).

For Charles and me, the consequences of that kerbside encounter were also far-reaching. Both of us faced a number of challenges in ministry in ensuing years and it was a great delight, comfort and privilege to be able to encourage and pray for one another through that time, either over the phone or at a later stage by email. Almost twenty years later, Charles visited the parish in which we were then serving and made an invaluable contribution in the year-long mission taking place, namely 'More to Life'* (see *Chocolate*), and I subsequently visited his church and university in Calgary, Canada.

The Feast of the Epiphany (the manifestation of Christ to the Gentiles) comes immediately after Christmas in the Church Year and marks the moment when the Christ Child is revealed to wise men from the east who have been led by a star to Bethlehem. The word 'epiphany' signifies 'the manifestation of the larger essence of something; an experience, often insignificant by itself, which illuminates a deeper, numinous foundation of reality'. In retrospect, Ruth would have seen her encounter with Boaz as an 'epiphany moment'

---

* An account and background to the mission can be read in *More to Life: A Model for Mission in the Local Church in the 21st Century*, No. 90, Evangelism Series, Grove Books, Cambridge.

and that is how the Nienkirchens and I see that kerbside encounter (on the Feast of the Epiphany!) in 1989.

The significance of such moments is that they can help us to see what previously had been unseen; they grant us a new perspective on life. They serve as a signpost to a greater reality.

What 'kerbside encounters' might you have today? Of course, they may not happen literally on a kerbside, such encounters can happen by the bedside, behind a desk, on a bus – anywhere.

'So she went out, and began to glean in the fields behind the harvesters. As it turned out, she found herself working in a field belonging to Boaz...'

Ruth 2:3

 LYING IN BED

> 'God understands our prayers even when we can't find the words to say them.'
>
> *Author unknown*

It was the middle of the January night in Guadalajara, Mexico, and my mother was lying in bed in acute pain. She was in Mexico visiting my sister Angela. Some years earlier Angela had met Miguel, a Mexican on study leave in London, and in due course they married and set up home in Mexico; before long their sons started arriving on the scene. Mum and Dad endeavoured to visit them once a year to keep in touch with the expanding family.

On this occasion, shortly after arriving, Mum contracted shingles on her face. Initially there was only minor discomfort but, after a week or two, the shingles became more painful and, disturbingly, entered her eyes. As a result, eye drops were required at four-hourly intervals, day and night. Before long, both Mum and Dad were exhausted.

Mum had always believed in God in a nominal manner – in the same way that if asked whether she thought the queen was alive she would unhesitatingly reply 'Yes', although until the moment the question was asked, she hadn't given the queen even a passing thought for days, if not weeks. Although she went to church on a fairly regular basis, Mum had no experience of a personal relationship with a loving God. Looking back, I can never remember her praying for us as children – I'm not saying that she didn't pray silently in her heart, rather that spoken prayer was never a part of our daily family routine.

In the depths of this Mexican night, Mum, in great pain and unable to sleep, felt moved to wonder whether she should (or, indeed, ought to) pray for God's help. In telling me later about this episode, Mum explained that she answered the question in her head with the response, 'Don't be absurd, Meg, what's the old fellow up there going to want with a clapped-out old bird like you? There are millions of people more worthy and needy than you in the world, millions who are starving, hurting and younger.'

However, such was the pain that Mum felt compelled to pray – with all the predictable caveats: 'I'm not asking for healing…' 'I'm sure I don't matter very much, but…' 'I don't want to use up your time on my problems…' and so on. In the event, at the end of her tether, Mum simply prayed, 'Dear God, please help me.'

At that moment, as soon as the words left her heart,

Mum sensed herself being drenched in a white light and just *knew* that God didn't merely 'love the whole world' (John 3:16) but that he loved Meg, this Meg lying on her bed in the middle of Mexico! Instantly that conviction – that God is a personal, relational, knowing and loving God – was bone deep.

Mum was not completely healed but, from that moment the pain lessened, the eye drops were effective and her anxiety vanished. When Dad awoke he saw a transformation in Mum's whole outlook, a transformation that lasted throughout the rest of their stay in Mexico. On their return, when we went to pick them up at Heathrow airport, Mum's face was almost healed and both Mum and Dad were full of all that had happened.

In the weeks that followed, Mum continued to speak joyfully and freely of her new sense of God's love that was an abiding presence each and every day. This included the Friday a few months later when, following a couple of weeks of stomach pains, she was admitted to Stoke Mandeville Hospital near Aylesbury.

It so happened that Bledlow Cricket Club, the village cricket team I played for, had a match in Aylesbury the next day – the only fixture of the season within miles of the hospital into which Mum had been admitted. Following the match, Chris and I were planning to drive down to Southampton with the children for a week's break and so we agreed that I'd leave the cricket at a timely moment so I could see Mum in hospital before we went on holiday.

Bledlow lost the toss and I spent the afternoon bowling and fielding, and then strolled into the pavilion for tea. As I wasn't batting till lower in the order, I decided to go to the hospital for a brief visit to Mum during the tea interval. It was only a short drive and, still wearing my cricket flannels, I soon arrived at her bedside in the ward. We had a very special time together and Mum expressed how at peace she felt, knowing the Lord's presence with her every moment. We briefly prayed together, I gave her a hug, and then drove back to the cricket match in time to bat.

'How was Mum, John?' enquired Chris. 'Well, put it this way,' I replied, 'if Mum were to die while we're in Southampton – which she won't because she is very settled and comfortable – I'd be completely at peace, knowing she is at peace with God and looking forward to heaven.'

The following Thursday, we were sitting around the breakfast table in Southampton when the phone rang. Mum had died suddenly, without any warning, early that morning. Notwithstanding the totally unexpected timing of the phone call and the news we received, the peace of God did indeed continue to engage our hearts, a peace that passed all understanding. We were held in that peace, in the sure and certain conviction that Mum was 'at home' in heaven with her loving God.

From the moment in the middle of that night in Guadalajara when Mum experienced the personal 'touch' of God's love for the first time in her life, at the age of sixty-eight, she continued to be held in his peace – through the remaining hours, days and months of her life. All it took was just one touch of God's love for one 'clapped-out old bird' (Mum's own words) to be at peace. How priceless is that!

> 'When I consider your heavens, the work of your fingers, the moon and the stars which you have set in place, what is mankind that you are mindful of them, human beings that you care for them?'
>
> *Psalm 8:3,4*

M4 MOTORWAY

'Coincidence is God's way of remaining anonymous.'

Albert Einstein

In September 1981 my cousin Michael and his wife, Janet, had invited my family and me to go to their silver wedding celebration in north-west London. We were living in Bristol, where I was studying at Trinity Theological College, and our two children, Roger and Jo, had just started their new term at school. Chris, my wife, wisely decided that the midweek evening would be far too late for the children and suggested I went on my own.

On the morning of the day in question I went into a bookshop in Bristol and, having found a book I was looking for, I queued up at the counter to pay. My eye caught a glimpse of a pile of car stickers beside the till and there was one I couldn't resist. For some weeks I had sensed the Lord challenging me to put a sticker on the car that spoke of my faith but, to be honest, I'd resisted the idea. My defence was that I found most of the stickers in question either insufferably pious or completely naff! On this occasion, however, I was drawn to one that simply declared: *Prayer changes things*. 'I can live with that,' I thought, and promptly bought one.

I returned to my car, attached the sticker to the rear window and returned home for lunch. Early in the afternoon I set off for the celebration. It was a great joy to meet up with my cousin's family but, as the evening drew on, I felt increasingly uneasy about the return drive that night, worrying that I might nod off as I drove down the M4 after such a long day.

Finally leaving the celebration at 10.45 p.m. I walked to the nearby car park, sending up a quick arrow prayer as I walked: 'Lord, I'm worried about falling asleep on the motorway; if you give me a hitchhiker to accompany me, I promise I'll share my faith with him.'

To be honest, I didn't think much more about it and set off for Junction 8/9 near Maidenhead, arriving at the junction at 11.25 p.m. To my amazement I saw two young men in army gear thumbing a lift. I pulled up and asked them where they were heading. 'Warminster,' they replied, and I said I could take them to the Warminster Road in Bath. 'Would that be OK?' 'Wonderful' they said and climbed in.

Smiling at the thought of my arrow prayer offered up forty-five minutes earlier, I asked them where they had started their journey. 'Southend,' they replied. 'How many lifts did it take you to get to Junction 8/9 and have you had much waiting around?' They explained they had had four lifts during the day, adding that the last fellow to give them a lift was 'a real nutter'. 'Goodness me,' I said, 'you've got to be so careful these days when you're hitch-hiking. What do you mean that he was a nutter?' 'Well,' they replied, 'he told us that he believed everything in the Bible was true!' Shifting rather uncomfortably in my seat, I replied, 'Well, lads, I think you've been picked up by another nutter!'

'Oh, no,' they said, 'it wasn't simply that he said he believed everything in the Bible was true. He told us that this very day he had bought a second-hand car and he was just putting it into his garage when he thought to himself, I wonder how fast this car can go? I'll give it a burst down the motorway and if I get the chance to pick up a hitch-hiker, even better – I'll share my faith in God with them.'

By now it was not far short of midnight on what had been, for me, a very long day but I have never ever been more wide-awake than I was at that moment! I said to them, 'You're not going to believe this, lads, but a little over an hour ago as I left a silver wedding celebration in Harrow and walked to the car, I sent up a prayer to the Lord asking him to give me a hitch-hiker wanting a lift down the motorway, to help me stay awake. You are the answer to that prayer!'

'Never!' said the two fellows. 'It's true,' I replied, 'just look over your shoulder and see what that sticker on the rear window says.' The headlights of the car behind lit it up. 'Prayer changes things', they said, incredulously.

It turned out that the first 'nutter' had left them at Junction 8/9 and they had been waiting there over half an hour for a lift. At that point, one of the lads had turned to the other and said 'That fellow told us that God answers prayer, let's pray for a lift.' They did so and a couple of minutes later a car drew up alongside them. One of them reached forward to open the door when the car suddenly accelerated away. 'It's your fault,' one said to the other, 'that chap said to us when we were laughing at him, "If you don't believe what I'm telling you that's your free choice, but don't mock the Lord or you'll be very sorry."' The car left the two lads standing sheepishly on the roadside and asking God (if he could hear them!) to forgive them and to bring another car along. It was just then that I pulled alongside them.

'So *what* do you believe?' asked the young men. I realised this was now a truly God-given opportunity to share my belief in God and his Word. When I had finished, the two men simply asked, 'Who told you all this stuff? It's just the same as that last chap was saying.' 'Well,' I replied, 'it's in the Bible, and I have found it to be true in every part of my life. Quite simply, my faith has turned my life upside-down, in a profoundly good way.'

By now we were driving along the A46 into Bath and I soon left the two lads on the Warminster Road before continuing to Bristol. I arrived home well after

1.30 p.m. and yet when I got into bed I could hardly sleep a wink!

How I would love to meet up with those two lads again. Perhaps one of them will pick up this book – if it's you, do please get in touch!

> 'The prayer of a person living right with God is something powerful to be reckoned with.'
>
> *James 5:16*, The Message

NIGERIA

'Where is the Life we have lost in living?
Where is the wisdom we have lost in knowledge?
Where is the knowledge we have lost in information?
The cycles of Heaven in twenty centuries
Bring us farther from God and nearer to the Dust.'
T. S. Eliot, from 'The Rock'

I didn't leave the shores of Great Britain until I was in my late teens. I don't regret this for one moment, for there is so much to explore and discover 'at home' and memories of holidays and journeys from those early years had a formative influence upon my life. However, as Kipling once observed, 'They that only England know, know not England', and approaching the end of my geography degree, I found myself undecided about what to do next. Considering various options, the one that most appealed was a year's service with Voluntary Service Overseas, an organisation that had been set up a few years earlier and which offered the opportunity to engage with a different culture. I duly applied and was accepted.

I discovered I was to be posted to Birnin Kebbi, a small town in the extreme north west of Nigeria, and in mid August 1966 I set off from Heathrow, bound for Africa, with a deep sense of excitement and some trepidation. How would I react to being beyond the reach of the telephone for one year; eating different food; engaging with local people in the Hausa language; living in the heat and aridity of the tropical savannah; experiencing the loss of being surrounded by cricket, rugby and football; the discovery of snakes in the surrounding countryside? A multitude of questions tumbled around in my head, including perhaps the most important one, indeed, the chief reason for taking this step: 'Would the path of life I should follow become clearer?'

Following an eight-hour night flight we landed in Kano, Nigeria, and those volunteers destined for the north of the country disembarked and stepped into the tropical heat of the early morning. Four of us were scheduled to go to Birnin Kebbi and we were picked up by a truck at the airport to begin the two-day journey to our destination. I discovered I was to share a house with Ron Dubbels, a Peace Corps volunteer from the Midwest of America, who was also teaching at the local secondary school. Ron was a committed Christian whereas I had recently turned away from the Christian faith following what can only be described as a 'reverse conversion experience' the previous Christmas at a midnight communion service (see *Introduction*).

The scene was set for some lively discussions as I settled in for the year and prepared myself for the impact that culture shock would have. Given the lack of facilities at the school and the limited amenities in Birnin Kebbi, which was about 95 miles from the nearest settlement of any size, Ron and I had plenty of time to reflect upon our individual reactions to the challenges the year presented – challenges associated with our health and diet, teaching at the school, engaging with the students and staff, exploring the local area, meeting with local people and taking the opportunity to travel during the school vacations.

In addition, discussions regarding matters of faith and politics (especially with USA involvement in Vietnam approaching its peak) were regularly on the agenda. Consequently, my hitherto settled values, established and shaped in 'middle England', were challenged at a number of levels. Questions began to occupy my mind, questions which before I had somewhat too easily brushed aside as I busily addressed the more immediate challenges and opportunities presented by sport, academic study and the social milieu. Suddenly, in a completely different world, my 'inner self' was being disturbed as I pondered a number of issues:

- The daily encounters in the school, on the streets, in the villages and at the markets. Each revealed a humour, vitality and openness which made the hard insularity of Western cultures seem absurd.

- Meeting the overflowing joy and positivity from people who had seemingly so little in their villages; saying 'hello' a hundred times a day; eye to eye contact and repeatedly shaking hands with all-comers. A quite different theology of touch was evident, contrasting with the English 'no touching/keep your distance' policy in so many encounters.

- Being constantly surprised and challenged by the daily sense of spontaneity (of hospitality and generosity) and social intimacy as barriers between strangers quickly came down, notably when encountering a group of nomadic herdsmen on the fringes of the desert early one morning. Eager for a photograph, I approached them with a camera and their one concern was to find something they could give me! All their worldly possessions were before me – a few cattle, three tents and some portable beds and tables – yet they were so desperate to share something. In the event they milked a cow and handed over a calabash of milk with endless smiles and laughter.

- Being constantly challenged by the local inhabitants' remarkable fortitude, exhibited in daily challenges and by the acceptance of death, even of close family members.

- Being reminded of my wastefulness by their determination to recycle as much as possible – for example, shoe polish tins being turned into cheese graters and rubber tyres into sandals.

- Having values brought into question by the leather worker – producing beautiful bags, wallets and cushions with the most basic of tools – who declined an opportunity to trade with a lucrative market overseas 'until he needed more money to enable his son to pay his wife's dowry for his wedding'. He was content with his lifestyle and, for him, money was only seen as a means to an end, not an end in itself – a rare perspective in our consumer-driven society and one that needs to be recovered following the excesses of the early twenty-first century.
- Gazing at the remarkable night skies in the silence and the absence of light pollution, with countless stars and constellations visible to the naked eye, I wondered 'what is my place in this universe?'
- Discovering, wholly unexpectedly, a deep love of teaching geography and sport, and engaging with young, open minds. It was the discovery of a true vocation.

Above all, Birnin Kebbi afforded me time to spend reflecting upon life's daily rhythms, encounters and experiences without the ever-present distraction of the television, social networking or the local pub!

It would be wrong to deny that at times it was difficult being so distant from friends and family. However, always I had it in mind that the reason for this period of dislocation was not mere escapism but rather that I should return to familiar territory with a clearer perspective on life's priorities. I wanted to know my 'home' and my place within it.

Culture shock can serve a valuable purpose. It can challenge our prejudices, often in an acutely uncomfortable way, questioning our settled values and judgements, making us 'think again' about all aspects of life. This is so important because prejudice is fatal to perception.

When Jesus declared to Nicodemus, 'I tell you the truth, unless a man is born again, he cannot see the kingdom of God' (John 3:3), he was making clear that we need to go back to 'square one' if we are to look at things afresh. Going to live in a foreign culture requires us to do just that. For me, above all, it was the relational integrity and openness I encountered in Nigeria that most challenged me.

This experience served to prepare me in due course to recognise and appreciate more fully God's greatest gift that is found at the very heart of the kingdom of God, namely a relational integrity rooted in 'agape' love.

P.S. I later returned to Nigeria with my wife, Chris, and son, Roger, so together we could share the experience. It was a decision that was to have a lasting impact upon our subsequent spiritual journeys.

> 'Blessed are those whose strength is in you, whose hearts are set on pilgrimage.'
>
> *Psalm 84:5*

ORANGE TIPS AND LARGE BLUES

'Beautiful and graceful, varied and enchanting, small but approachable, butterflies lead you to the sunny side of life. And everyone deserves a little sunshine.'

Jeffrey Glassberg

Butterflies have held a fascination for me since I was seven years old. One day our next-door neighbour presented me with a matchbox containing a Peacock butterfly which had overwintered in their garage and had died in the cold. I was at once totally absorbed by its beauty and apparent fragility. On that day an interest began that has never waned and every summer has offered hours of delight seeking out and observing these beautiful 'aerial flowers'.

As a youngster I already had a perfunctory belief in God, but it was the wonder of design evident in butterflies that served to awaken in me a new awareness of the intricacy in God's creation. The more I discovered about butterflies the more astonished I became. As I read Richard South's book *The Butterflies of the British Isles*, more and more remarkable details emerged.

I soon discovered that the colour on butterfly wings easily rubs off when touched, leaving a 'dust' on your finger tip that resembles fine talcum powder. Intrigued as I was that such coloured 'dust' is distributed so precisely upon the wings, under a microscope much more interesting facts began to emerge. Each speck of dust is in reality a flattened bag like a scale, attached by a stalk on the membrane of the wing. Amazingly, the arrangement of the scales resembles the slates on a roof, each overlapping the next. The colour is chiefly due to pigment contained in each scale and is established while the butterfly is still only a chrysalis. Such extraordinary detail and design!

Each year, when I catch my first glimpse in the hedgerows of a wild flower known both as Lady's Smock or Cuckoo Flower, usually towards the end of April, I am reminded of the astonishing connectedness within the world that God has created. This particular flower is the food plant of the Orange Tip butterfly, one of the earliest to emerge in the spring. Orange Tips are beautiful and carry with them the promise of summer. As the name implies, the butterfly (or at least the male) has a large patch of deep orange on the outer third of its creamy white forewings, and the extreme tip is blackish. On the female a smaller, blackish-grey patch replaces the orange one. Orange Tip butterflies feed on the nectar provided by Lady's Smock flowers and lay their eggs on the stalks, the resulting caterpillars feeding on the leaves. Each year I find it a source of wonder to witness the almost simultaneous arrival of food plant and insect. Whenever I see my first Orange Tip I look for the flowers of Lady's Smock nearby; alternatively, if I first see the Lady's Smock in flower, I am on the alert for an Orange Tip on the wing and I am reminded of these words: 'You prepare a table before me in the presence of my enemies' (Psalm 23:5).

Even more remarkable is the life cycle of the rare Large Blue butterfly. Having become extinct in the UK in the late 1970s, the butterfly was reintroduced in the 1990s using a Scandinavian species that most closely resembled the lost UK species. A successful conservation programme is now well established and its success is due to the intricate discoveries made about the life cycle and the particular demands of the butterfly at each stage of its development.

The Large Blue butterfly emerges in mid June and lays its eggs on wild thyme buds, the butterfly feeding from the nectar in the thyme flowers. The resulting caterpillars feed on the flowers and, when well fed, the caterpillar secretes a sweet fluid which attracts a particular species of red ant, *Mymirca sabuleti*. The red ant first strokes the caterpillar with its antenna, making it produce drops of honeydew, and then picks the caterpillar up in its jaws and takes it back to the ant nest.

There, the ant continues to stroke the caterpillar, feeding from the honeydew, while the caterpillar mimics red ant sounds to make it less of a threat to the ants. In time, the caterpillar makes its way to the ants' nesting chamber and feeds from the red ant eggs and larvae, before hanging by its legs from the roof, turning into a chrysalis and hibernating for the winter. Once inside the chrysalis, the caterpillar scrapes against the wall of the chrysalis making the sound a red ant makes, otherwise the red ant would eat it!

After transforming underground into a butterfly in June, the butterfly is escorted to the surface by the red ants and led to a nearby flower. The red ants encircle the butterfly to ward off any predators that might attack the butterfly before its wings have dried out and enlarged. The butterfly is then ready to fly off, find a mate and repeat the egg-laying cycle. The butterfly remains on the wing for perhaps three weeks before it dies.

The extraordinary, detailed requirements of the butterfly from its egg to maturity were only realised as the conservation programme progressed. In particular, the Large Blue requires a south-facing hillside with close-cropped, unfertilised pasture, the precise length of the grass being crucial for the creation of the appropriate micro climate to support the particular species of red ant required.

The complexity of the habitat required for the Large Blue to be successfully established is remarkable. Is all of this by chance or by design? Such a question leads us to the inevitable debate which has polarised opinion for a long, long time: 'Is it evolution or creation?'

Sadly, often as a result of inadequate scientific and theological reasoning, the ensuing argument generates far more heat than light, for there is evidence of the possible coexistence of evolution and creation. This evidence is provided both in the natural world and in the Bible.

In the first chapter of Genesis, in which the creation of the world is so poetically described, different verbs are included in the process, *'bara'* (verses 1, 21, 27), *'dasha'* (verse 11), *'yatsa'* (verses 12, 24) and *'sharats'* (verses 20, 21). *Bara* refers to creating something from nothing, a quantum leap such as animate from inanimate, while *dasha*, *yatsa* and *sharats* refer to a remodelling or reshaping. Thus the argument regarding the relative merits of creation and evolution, invariably associated with a defining statement of faith (or lack of it), creates a false division. Both coexist in the natural world, which bears the mark of a creator and provides room for adaption or evolution. For me, the world of butterflies offers a fascinating insight into this important truth.

As the Elizabethan scientist Francis Bacon perceptively observed, 'God has written two books: the book of words, the Bible, and the book of works, creation. We need to read both if we are to discover the nature and purposes of God.'

'How many are your works, Lord! In wisdom you made them all; the earth is full of your creatures... All creatures look to you to give them their food at the proper time.'

Psalm 104:24, 27

PRISON

'Freedom is the oxygen of the soul.'

Moshe Dayan

Her Majesty's Prison Bristol was established during the 1880s and is one of the earliest prisons built by the Prison Commissioners. While most of the buildings on the site were built in the twentieth century, the surviving early buildings consist of a large prison wing and, until recently, housed the chapel. It was in this chapel, on a wet and windy winter Sunday morning, that a life-changing encounter took place in 1982.

From the time when I was a young boy, prisons have held a fascination for me. When we went on family holidays to Devon in my childhood, the holiday always seemed to include a journey through Princetown where we set eyes upon the infamous Dartmoor Prison. Once we even saw a group of prisoners being led back to the prison from a day's work in the local quarries – excitement indeed for a young lad!

Several years later in 1981, when I discovered that one of the options available in the course of ordination training was a pastoral placement at HMP Bristol, I was particularly interested in taking up the opportunity. The subsequent experience was to prove very beneficial in parochial ministry because in each of the parishes in which I subsequently served there were families with personal connections with the prison system. In addition, in the course of my visits to the prison, a story unfolded which had life-changing consequences for one of the prisoners.

Phil, a former serviceman, was serving a relatively short sentence for a couple of years, and one day, having visited him a few times, I shared with him the story surrounding a tragic and relatively recent railway accident (see *Tragedy*). The story visibly moved Phil deeply and we began to talk about ways in which God can meet us in difficult circumstances. At the end of the visit, I felt moved to ask him whether he would like to come to chapel one Sunday and to my delight he said he would. It happened I had a free Sunday ten days later so we arranged to meet up for the morning service then.

Neither of us had been to the prison chapel before and immediately we entered I was struck by the high windows in the Victorian building. The prisoners shuffled in, clearly relishing the opportunity for a time outside their cells and the chance to chat to their fellow inmates; for some, the fact that the gathering happened in the chapel was purely coincidental!

Phil and I walked in and sat at the end of a row of chairs, near to the windows. Wind and rain 'lashed' against the windows and it was comforting to be in the warmth of the chapel. A group of young musicians was setting up their instruments, preparing to lead the service; the female lead singer was stunningly attractive and she was certainly gaining the interest of many prisoners as they sat down.

My attention was drawn elsewhere. The group was called 'New Beginnings' and I couldn't help noticing that all their instruments had a butterfly painted on them – a symbol of their faith and belief that new life is offered to all who received Christ into their hearts. In the light of the story I had shared with Phil about the railway tragedy, I nudged him and commented on the butterfly. He nodded and said he hadn't missed it!

As the service continued, it was noticeable that many of the prisoners used the noise of the hymn singing to mask their conversations with fellow inmates; they seemingly had little interest in proceedings in the chapel. However, that changed as 'New Beginnings' began to share their story, notably when they sang a song entitled 'The Father's Love'. The song had been written by the group after a few days they had recently spent together on a visit to a Young Offenders' Institute, and it spoke of the love in God's heart for each and every one of us, particularly those with broken lives and on the margins of society. Gradually the murmuring stopped and everyone in the chapel was held in rapt attention. Prisoners and officers alike listened intently as the group sang of the cry of God's heart for all people, including those who knew they had screwed up their life.

It was at this precise moment that, out of the corner of my eye, I saw a butterfly flutter up the inside of a window (as the wind and rain continued to beat on the outside) just by the end of the row in which Phil and I were sitting. I prayed that Phil would see this as he listened to the ache of God's heart for the lost, so movingly expressed in music.

I needn't have worried. At the end of the service, the group invited anyone in the chapel who wanted to respond to God's love to come forward, and nothing would have kept Phil from going forward to pray a prayer of repentance and ask God into his life. Shortly afterwards we returned to Phil's cell, where I prayed with him, and then returned home praising God for the remarkable way so many things had come together that morning.

A few months later, Phil was released from prison. As I stood outside waiting for him to come through the gates at 7.10 a.m, he suddenly appeared and walked straight across the road to shake my hand. 'John,' he said, 'I want to thank God for bringing me to this place, because it is here I have truly met with him.' Again, we prayed briefly and then Phil set off to be reunited with his family.

That episode happened thirty years ago. Every

Christmas Day since then (with one exception)* at 1.00 p.m. our phone has rung and it has been Phil calling to share what has been going on in his family's life and to recall our meeting those many years ago.

I have only met Phil twice since the day he was released from prison. The first time was when I returned to the Vicarage having taken an 8.00 a.m. Holy Communion service in St Aldate's Church, Oxford. I opened the front door and heard a man's voice inside. Intrigued, I walked into the kitchen and there was Phil talking with my family – he was en route to visit his mother in Gloucestershire and, on the spur of the moment, had decided to drop in to see us. We persuaded him to come to the morning service and, to our incredulity and joy, hanging in the front of the

---

* On Christmas Day in 2012 Chris and I were visiting our daughter, Jo, and her family at the school in Kenya where they were teaching. Shortly after lunch, Chris said, 'We'll miss Phil's call!'

Not long after our return, while we were still catching up with unanswered letters, the phone rang, on the evening of Monday 21 January 2013, and it was Phil! He explained he had rung several times over Christmas and the New Year, realised we must be away and decided to ring later in the month. It was such a joy to touch base with him once again and, towards the end of the conversation, Phil said these words: 'I always come away from the phone after speaking to you, John, with a deep sense of peace and the conviction that, whatever happens to me in this world, there is someone going to look after me in my hour of need. Indeed, our conversations always bring to my mind the poem "Footprints" – reminding me that in my deepest hour of need, God was indeed carrying me!'

God's fingerprint was clearly laid upon Phil's life through that encounter in prison!

church that morning (for the first time) was a huge banner covered in butterflies! Only the previous Wednesday our house group had decided to make it for the church, having spent a couple of meetings reflecting on the verse 'If anyone is in Christ, he is a new creation; the old has gone, and the new has come' (2 Corinthians 5:17).

That remarkable morning only served to underline the unforgettable events which had happened in prison so many years earlier. Truly, 'all things hold together in him'!

'The Spirit of the Sovereign Lord is on me, because the Lord has anointed me to proclaim good news to the poor. He has sent me to bind up the broken-hearted, to proclaim freedom for the captives and release from darkness for the prisoners…'

Isaiah 61:1

QUESTIONS

What is the most important, dangerous question you've ever asked? For myself, I think back to the afternoon of 20 January in 1968 when I was sitting in an armchair, watching England play Wales at Twickenham. When the referee blew the half-time whistle, I turned to the attractive young lady sitting in the chair next to me, my girlfriend of over two years, and asked, 'Chris, will you marry me?' It doesn't get any more important, or dangerous, than that! Thankfully her response, in a word, was 'Yes!'

The score at half time was 0–0: the final score 11–11. Clearly the second half was full of incident and nail-biting tension but, to be honest, I cannot remember anything about it – and, yes, we were still watching the match! What I do know is that Chris's response to my question opened the door to a new realm of life with far-reaching consequences that neither of us could have ever imagined.

Not for a moment am I suggesting it was easy to ask that question, but avoiding questions – both asking and answering them – significantly diminishes our quality of life.

What is the most important question you have ever *been* asked? For me it was the moment when I was talking with the Revd Dr Michael Green who had been invited to speak during an evening guest service held at our local church in High Wycombe. I was a geography teacher at the time and for a number of years had been exploring my spiritual journey, becoming increasingly convinced of the existence of a living God.

Several years earlier Michael and I had been members of the same local cricket team and it was a joy to meet up with him once again. Towards the end of our conversation reminiscing over old times, he asked me, 'Do you know the Lord?' As it turned out, that was the most important question I have ever been asked. At that moment, I had to face up openly to my relationship with God. Was it merely a propositional truth, a belief in a relationship that I simply privatised and kept in my head, or was this relationship with Jesus one that was going to shape the whole of my outlook on life?

'Yes,' I replied, and immediately Michael responded by praying for me and Chris, who was standing beside me, asking God to fill us with his Spirit and guide us clearly along the path that would lead us to life in all its fullness.

As Chris and I walked home from church we

realised something profoundly significant had happened that evening. Having said that I 'knew the Lord' and recognising that my spiritual journey would inevitably impact upon our family, we resolved from that night onwards to pray and read the Bible together on a daily basis. By the grace of God, the commitment we made that night has been sustained and has served to shape our lives ever since. It was a commitment that sprang from the right question being asked, and answered, at the right time.

The great political and spiritual leader Mahatma Gandhi observed that 'the power to question is the basis of all human progress'. Good questions can engage people, make them feel valued, build trust and deepen relationships. Questions serve to provide information and to bring about transformation, both of which are crucial elements in building relationships – with others and with God.

In view of this, it's hardly surprising that questions should play such a key role in the life and ministry of Jesus. In fact his earliest recorded words in his life, found in the Gospel of Luke, are phrased in two questions addressed to his parents, who had been anxiously searching for their twelve-year-old son in Jerusalem. Having lost him on their return journey from the Feast of the Passover, it took them some time to find him '…in the temple courts, sitting among the teachers, listening to them and asking them questions. Everyone who heard him was amazed at his understanding and his answers. When his parents saw him, they were astonished. His mother said to him, "Son, why have you treated us like this? Your father and I have been anxiously searching for you." "Why were you searching for me?" he asked. "Didn't you know I had to be about my Father's business?" But they did not understand what he was saying to them' (Luke 2:46–50).

I'm sure this incident sends a shudder down many a reader's back as we recall the time we 'lost' our child in the supermarket or on the beach! Luke records that Jesus' parents didn't understand what he was saying to them but, once they had calmed down, I'm sure those questions Jesus posed caused them to think afresh about their son – especially his second question, 'Didn't you know I had to be about my Father's business?' This very neatly summarises the agenda that would dominate every hour of Jesus' life, a truth that John records clearly in his Gospel. 'Jesus gave… this answer: "Very truly I tell you, the Son can do nothing by himself; he can only do what he sees his Father doing, because whatever the Father does the Son also does"' (John 5:19).

Throughout his ministry, Jesus sought to fulfil the will of his Heavenly Father and encouraged those who choose to follow him to have the same agenda. The use of questions – questions designed not merely to impart information but also to bring about transformation among his disciples – played a key role in his teaching. The key to powerful thinking is powerful questioning, and Jesus certainly wanted his disciples to think deeply about their faith because he was aware they would face a host of tricky questions from those who doubted his claims. It is no different today!

One formula you may find useful for identifying important questions is known as W5H, which stands for 'What? Why? Where? When? Who?' and 'How'. It is fascinating to see how Jesus and those seeking to follow him freely tossed W5H questions around. Consider the following:

'How can someone be born when they are old?' (John 3:4)

'My God, my God, why have you forsaken me?' (Mark 15:34)

'Who do you say I am?' (Mark 8:29)

'Teacher, which is the greatest commandment in the Law?' (Matthew 22:36)

'What sign then will you give that we may see it and believe you? (John 6:30)

'Where did this man get this wisdom and these miraculous powers? (Matthew 13:54)

Perhaps the two most important questions Jesus addresses to those who seek to follow him are the following: 'Who do you say I am?' (Mark 8:29) and 'What do you want me to do for you?'(Mark 10:51). Do not dismiss these last two questions too quickly and jump to hasty conclusions, for both can serve as important signposts on one's spiritual journey. In response to the first, read a modern translation of one of the gospels (I suggest Mark or John) in a measured way, perhaps with a friend or two, and reflect on what strikes you about Jesus. In response to the second, ponder what would serve to make your life more fulfilling, because the one who asks the question also states, 'I have come… that you might have life – life in all its fullness' (John 10:10, Good News Translation).

Life is too short to let these two questions pass us by.

> 'Jesus and his disciples went on to the villages around Caesarea Philippi. On the way he asked them, "Who do people say I am?" They replied, "Some say John the Baptist; others say Elijah; and still others, one of the prophets." "But what about you?" he asked. "Who do you say I am?"
>
> *Mark 8:27–29*

ROBIN

'I believe in prayer; it is the best way we have to draw strength from heaven'

Josephine Baker

It's curious, isn't it, how some fleeting moments are indelibly imprinted on our minds. Some are widely shared, such as recalling the place and time we first heard the news of J. F. Kennedy's assassination or 9/11; others are much more personal, but no less significant in their impact on our lives.

Time: One morning in May 1982.

Place: Outside the front entrance of Trinity Theological College, Bristol.

Robin and I bumped into each other as we arrived at college for morning prayers and lectures. He was shortly to complete his two years of theological training, leave Bristol and enter his first parish as a curate. I greeted him with a cheery 'Morning, Robin! How are you?' and he replied, 'I'm fine… In fact, yesterday, I had an extraordinary encounter with God.' 'Really?' I replied, 'Tell me what happened.'

As Robin recounted the events of the previous day, I listened with growing incredulity, and I have retold this episode many times over the past thirty years. Not least it has served to shape the way I have prepared for daily tasks.

The previous morning, Robin had woken up after a fitful night's sleep and pondered the day before him. A seeming nightmare lay ahead of him and, humanly speaking, it looked impossible to negotiate. Robin's wife, Sue, feeling very unwell, was confined to bed and unable to contribute anything to the daily routine; Robert and Janice, their two teenage children, were immersed in exam preparation and also needed to be taken to different parts of Bristol at inconvenient, conflicting times; Robin had two essays to complete by the middle of the next week and, in addition, was feeling anxious about the fast-approaching departure from college and entry into ministry. To cap it all, there was shopping to be done!

As he lay there, Robin felt paralysed by the prospect of the day that lay ahead of him. He clambered out of bed, got washed and dressed, and brewed a cup of tea. His morning quiet time beckoned and, so heavily was the day weighing upon him, Robin decided not simply to sit in a chair but rather to kneel down and clasp his hands together in what was, for him, a rather formal posture.

Having offered thanks to God for the gift of a new day and the assurance of his love and grace, Robin tried to prioritise the concerns whirling around inside his head. 'Who should I pray for first – my wife, my children, wider concerns in the world… surely not my own needs?' As Robin pondered these thoughts, holding an internal conversation with himself, in the quiet he suddenly 'heard' God say to him, 'Robin, I've got all the power in the world. How much do you want?'

Robin found himself opening his clasped hands a bit and saying, 'Well, Lord, if you give me this amount, that will take care of my wife and then I'll be able to see to the children and face the other pressing needs of the day.' Robin felt a jump in his hands and then heard God say once more, 'Do you want some more, Robin? I've got it all.'

Robin opened his hands wider and responded, 'Thank you, Lord, if I can have that much it will see to the needs of my wife, Robert and Janice and, knowing their needs will be met, I'll be able to face the other demands of the day.' By now Robin had been in prayer for over twenty minutes and was beginning to anticipate the day ahead much more positively. But each time he paused to consider what his next prayer should be, all Robin heard was God responding, 'Is that all you need, Robin?'

Finally, with his arms stretched out almost horizontally, Robin replied, 'But Lord, I can only stretch out this far,' as he strained to extend his arms to the fullest extent. At that moment he sensed the Lord replying, 'Yes, Robin, that is what I've done for you so that you can have all of me. Who are you to think you can go into any day without all of me?' Immediately, Robin was reminded of the words that the apostle Paul wrote to the church in Galatia: 'I have been crucified with Christ and I no longer live, but Christ lives in me' (Galatians 2:20).

For some time, as his training began to draw to a close and his ordination drew nearer, Robin had been sensing a growing reluctance to leave college, a fear of being 'launched' into ministry. Now, as he knelt, he was prompted to bring these doubts before God, admitting, 'Lord, I don't think I've got what it takes to serve you.' As he paused to gather the thoughts and doubts swirling around in his mind, he sensed God replying, 'Robin, I have all that you need,' accompanied by a deep assurance.

In due course, Robin completed his prayer time, got to his feet and prepared to enter the day, no longer uncertainly but now with a deep sense of God's presence and promise. In the event, the day passed much more smoothly than Robin could have ever imagined and he was left reflecting upon his total dependency on the grace of God, not merely at college but throughout his forthcoming ministry and, indeed, in each and every aspect of his life.

Thirty years after that morning encounter at the entrance to Trinity College, I contacted Robin by telephone; not having spoken to him since the day he left college. At once he recalled the day in question and, as we reflected together on 'life in the parish', it was clear that the experience during that prayer time had deeply shaped the whole of his ministry.

From that May morning in 1982 onwards, it has shaped my ministry, too. In particular I have found adopting the posture of kneeling and stretching out my hands, as a reminder of my complete dependency upon the Lord, profoundly energising. Decades later, before a meeting or sermon, I still frequently find myself kneeling and stretching out my arms, praying for the Lord to release his grace afresh upon me. The physical act of fully stretching out, as a reminder of what Jesus did for me upon the Cross, and inviting the Holy Spirit to fill every nook and cranny of my being, is both fortifying and liberating. It serves to remind me that 'I no longer live, but Christ lives in me' (Galatians 2:20) and that Jesus is the one to be glorified, because of what he has done for me… and for each one of us.

How thankful I am to God for that encounter with Robin!

> 'I can do all this through him who gives me strength… And my God will meet all your needs according to the riches of his glory in Christ Jesus. To our God and Father be glory for ever and ever. Amen.'
>
> *Philippians 4:13,19,20*

SNOW AND SILENCE

'Snow is the ultimate marriage of complexity in harmony. Billions upon billions of unique notes fall together in a crescendo of white unity. If you should ever be blessed to be far enough from the crush of civilization when a heavy snow falls, you can even hear the very music of the iced dew's delicate descent. It is the repainting of a landscape, in a thousand hues of white. It is the very dance of the wind. It is as if, just for a time, we get to enter the wonder of Narnia, or of Middle Earth, to dance amidst the miracle of liquid manna. It is falling snow that invites us to be still and know that He is God.'

R.C. Sproul Jr

I have to admit it – I love snow, and have done as long as I can remember. As a boy, elbows on the windowsill and head in my hands, I'd be waiting for my first winter glimpse of the 'white stuff'. Even if you detest snow –

the fear of skidding and falling on the pavements, the prospect of shovelling, delays, slush and all the associated inconvenience – the first accumulation is so beautiful, the world overtaken with breathless wonder and beauty. For a moment, cars are stilled and the world sleeps in the silence of the snowfall.

Silence and wonder are almost lost in the developed world in which humankind has spent so much time advancing the technique of living at the expense of the art of living. How we need a renaissance of wonder in the journey of life! The sense of wonder is one of the saving graces; it evokes a thirst for discovery and without it we might just as well be dead. Yet, sadly, the reality is that as the years pass our sense of wonder so frequently shrivels and is replaced by a worldly cynicism. No matter how beautiful the day, how long will it be before we hear the gruff comment, 'It won't last'?

Within each one of us lies an innate sense of wonder which one can be readily reminded of when walking with a child. In many ways we do not show children the world, rather they reveal it afresh to us: taking delight in the antics of a worm, catching a falling leaf, smelling the scent of a flower, peering under a stone… Of course, all this takes up 'precious' time, a scarce commodity amid the hurly-burly and busyness of life. Perhaps it's not surprising that a sense of wonder and the gift of silence are increasingly rare commodities for which so many of us yearn. American poet Lawrence Ferlinghetti neatly expresses this in his poem 'I am waiting': '… I am awaiting/ perpetually and forever/ a renaissance of wonder'.

This is why snow, in particular the awakening dawn after a night's snowfall, is such a gift to our society, notwithstanding the difficulties it can generate. Ahead await the perils of negotiating the pavements, steering the car, reaching the shops, but just for a moment as the world awakens, our senses delight in discovering the wondrous 'repainting' of the landscape.

Snow is intrinsically a thing of wonder. A super-cooled water droplet freezes on to a dust particle or other cloud nucleus and forms an ice crystal, the precise shape of which is determined by the humidity of the air and atmospheric temperature. As they fall through the atmosphere and are carried by air currents, the ice crystals combine into flakes and form the most intricate, beautiful designs, the unique beauty of each flake shaped by the path it has taken and the meteorological environment through which it has travelled. Snowflakes accumulate in an airy arrangement that readily reflects all colours of the light spectrum, which not only explains the brightness of the light associated with snow but also the wholly unexpected possibility of sunburn from reflected sun's rays.

The transformation of the landscape is immediate – suddenly everything is clean, white and pure. It is intriguing that in the Old Testament, Isaiah records these words: 'Though your sins are like scarlet, they shall be as white as snow' (Isaiah 1:18). The word used for scarlet refers to an indelible dye, one that cannot be erased. In the same way that it would be impossible for us to 'repaint the landscape' in the manner of an overnight snowfall, so too is it impossible for us to 'blot out' our sins. Jesus Christ has achieved this transformation for us through his own sacrifice on the Cross, whereby he 'loves us and washed us from our sin by his blood' (Revelation 1:5, NRSV). Truly wondrous!

The following story shares that sense of wonder and illustrates the significance of that picture of our sins being washed away by the blood of Jesus. One day a man was driving his lorry laden with animals to a local slaughterhouse when the vehicle broke down. The driver's hands became covered in all kinds of grease and dirt while he carried out repairs and he apologised for their filthy state on arrival at the slaughterhouse. The men working there laughed and pointed to a nearby tank into which blood from carcasses had been drained. 'Dip your hands in there, give them a rub, and see the result,' they said. Sceptically the driver followed their suggestion and was astonished to discover his hands were spotless when they emerged from the blood. He had discovered that blood is the finest natural cleansing agent!

The significance and depth of those words of Isaiah come alive in a fresh way. What extraordinary cleansing power there is in blood, most especially in the shed blood of Jesus!

'...If we walk in the light, as he is in the light, we have fellowship with one another, and the blood of Jesus, his Son, purifies us from all sin.'

I John 1:7

TRAGEDY

The phone rang, breaking the quiet of the evening. I was about to learn of a tragic accident that had cost the lives of two young lads. Each attended the Royal Grammar School (RGS), High Wycombe, where I had taught until a few months earlier, and Ian Clark, a dear friend and former colleague, had rung to tell me the news…

It was at 8.14 a.m. on Friday 11 December 1981 when tragedy struck. Heavy snow had fallen unseasonably early in recent days and overnight there had been a further fall in the Chiltern Hills. The driver of the 7.31 train from Marylebone Station in London, heading for Banbury, was at Gerrards Cross Station when the signalman advised him that the snow had weighed down a number of branches hanging over the railway line to High Wycombe.

Unknown to either of them ahead lay a stationary, empty train. Its driver, having told the signalman at High Wycombe that a branch had broken off a tree and was blocking the line, had climbed out to move the obstruction. Meanwhile, in Gerrards Cross, passengers boarded the train from Marylebone and set off towards High Wycombe. With vision impaired by the heavy snow, the driver had no idea there was a problem on the track ahead, and at Seer Green there was a collision. The front coach was crushed under the rear of the empty train, killing the driver and three passengers.

Two of those passengers were promising young students setting off for another day at school, Andrew Russell and Nicholas McManus. A committed Christian, Andrew had a routine, including a Bible reading, which he followed each morning before setting off to school. That morning he had been reading the following passage from the Bible:

'Since, then, you have been raised with Christ, set your hearts on things above, where Christ is seated at the right hand of God. Set your minds on things above, not on earthly things. For you died, and your life is now hidden with Christ in God. When Christ, who is your life, appears, then you also will appear with him in glory' (Colossians 3:1–3).

Alongside these printed words was a picture of a butterfly, representing the new life we have in Christ.

Having put his Bible notes down on his bedside table, Andrew had his breakfast, collected his things for school, put on his thick winter coat and gloves, and set off to catch the train to school, meeting Nicholas McManus at Gerrards Cross station. They climbed aboard into the front coach…

It was several hours before the families were informed of the tragic events. In the conversations that followed profound grief being shared, Andrew's parents talked of the Bible reading their son had completed before the fateful journey and mentioned the accompanying butterfly picture. The following morning, with snow still deep on the ground and an icy wind blowing, Nicholas' mother went into her son's bedroom, still deep in shock. As she entered the room it was with incredulity that she saw, flying just above Nicholas' pillow, a butterfly!

Immediately, Nicholas' mother got in touch with Andrew's parents to tell them what had happened. Intuitively, in a deep, deep way, both families were united in the conviction, despite their grief, that their sons were safe in heaven with Jesus. Huge questions remained for the families to come to terms with in the weeks and years that lay ahead but now those questions were underpinned by a living, enduring hope. This was conveyed on the service card that was produced for Andrew's funeral, in which the words were printed on the background of a butterfly in flight.

The particular circumstances and details of this story have brought comfort and hope to countless people in the ensuing years (see *Prison*). One notable instance followed a tragedy in the midst of New Year's Eve 2003 in Scotland. A young girl, Laura, was staying overnight with her grandmother and during the late evening there was a power cut, resulting in some candles being lit. In time, one of them was somehow dislodged and caused a cushion to start smouldering while Laura and her grandmother had nodded off. Before long the house was filled with smoke and both the girl and her grandmother died from asphyxiation.

Laura's family lived in the parish in Keynsham, near Bristol, where I was vicar. One evening before the funeral for Laura, which was to be held in the parish church, I visited the family to share in their grief and to pray with them. During the conversation, one of the images I used was to describe the resurrection hope that we have in Jesus as being likened to the transformation of a caterpillar into a butterfly as it emerges from a chrysalis. I recounted the story of the train crash and how the incident with the butterfly had brought such hope to the families. Laura' parents, Heather and Pete, together with Laura's two sisters, Donna and Faye, found the story comforting in the midst of their grief.

The day of the funeral dawned bright and sunny, and bitterly cold. A strong north-east wind was blowing and mourners were dressed warmly against the cold as they arrived at the church. The funeral hearse arrived outside the church and, with the congregation seated, the pall-bearers carried the coffin to the church entrance. I invited the congregation to stand and led the coffin in. Before I had walked five paces down the aisle I suddenly caught sight of a butterfly coming down from the roof of the church towards the coffin. As Pete, Heather, Donna and Faye followed the coffin, they too saw the butterfly, which, to their incredulity, settled on the coffin and remained there throughout the service. Immediately the family's thoughts went back to the story I had shared with them just a few days earlier.

Following the service and burial, Heather, Pete and the girls all commented on the butterfly that they had encountered when walking down the aisle and, in the following months, as they worked out their understanding and acceptance of the tragic New Year events, butterflies became a very significant sign of hope for them.

They are not alone in that belief.

> 'Jesus cried out… "My God, my God, why have you forsaken me?"'
>
> *Matthew 27:46*

UNIVERSE

> 'There they stand, the innumerable stars, shining in order like a living hymn, written in light.'
>
> *N. P. Willis*

Humans have been looking up into the night skies in a search for meaning since they first stepped out on to the African savannah. I arrived in the savannah region of rural northern Nigeria less than forty-eight hours after leaving the hustle and bustle of suburban London and was immediately struck by the stunning beauty of the night skies. Watching the sky at night for any length of time is not easy in our hectic, well-lit world but in the African bush, with few distractions and frequent power cuts, an hour or two spent gazing at the heavens never loses its allure. I had come to Africa to spend a year working as a volunteer with a desire to lose myself in another culture and, in so doing, to 'find' myself.

As I busied myself with settling in to my new surroundings, my heart and mind were full of many questions and I realised I needed to discover a new, clear sense of perspective. The hours spent gazing at the heavens ablaze with stars, cloudless for months and free from light pollution, served a crucial role in my quest for meaning. The stars served as a timeless tutor, the sheer magnitude of the African skies, and the awe and wonder they evoked, generating a sense of humility in my heart. I began to wonder, 'What is my place in the midst of this grandeur?'

When one investigates the scale of the universe, the sense of awe and wonder only increases. The universe consists of billions and billions of galaxies and each galaxy itself contains many billions of stars. The Milky Way galaxy, the one Planet Earth inhabits, comprises more than 300 billion stars, including the one we orbit – the Sun, Yet if, for example, the Earth were a sphere the size of a golf ball, the size of the Sun would be a sphere with a fifteen-foot diameter and the largest known star in the Milky Way galaxy, the crimson *Canis Majorus*, would be a sphere with a diameter of six miles!

Advances in technology, notably the creation of the Hubble space telescope, have yielded many remarkable views and insights into the universe we inhabit, not least proving the existence of 'black holes', formed when massive stars collapse at the end of their life cycle. These black holes are regions of space–time from which nothing, not even light, can escape because of their immense gravitational pull. Apparently, a black hole the size of a London bus could swallow up a whole galaxy! How can this be?

Over time a black hole merges with other black holes to form the 'super-massive black hole' which is believed to exist in the centre of most galaxies. Remarkably, the Hubble space telescope revealed that the huge black hole at the heart of the Milky Way is shaped like a cross! Given the extraordinary power attributed to black holes, this image perhaps helps us to understand, in a fresh way, how the Cross of Calvary could possess the power to consume 'the sins of the whole world'.

Looking up at the starry skies, the psalmist, familiar with caring for his sheep, wrote, 'By the word of the Lord were the heavens made, their starry host by the breath of his mouth' (Psalm 33:6). Reflecting on these words in the light of our current understanding about the universe offers a new perspective on a star-breathing, cross-bearing God!

It is impossible to ponder the sight and scale of the universe without a sense of awe and wonder. The poet Edward Young (1683–1775) reflected that 'wonder is involuntary praise', and as I sat reflecting on the beauty and majesty stretched out above sub-Saharan Africa, I found myself inwardly expressing praise and reflecting deeply on the origins and purpose of life itself. Young is also attributed with saying, 'by night an atheist half believes in God', a perfect summation of the way in which my inner journey was beginning to unfold. The journey to faith invariably embraces a number of stages and signposts, and the starry vista arrayed in the night skies of Africa was certainly one for me.

Indeed it is a star embedded in the familiar Christmas story recounting the journey of the wise men that leads them to the King. 'After Jesus was born in Bethlehem in Judea, during the time of King Herod, Magi from the east came to Jerusalem and asked, "Where is the one who has been born king of the Jews? We have come to worship him." … they went on their way, and the star they had seen in the east went ahead of them until it stopped over the place where the child was. When they saw the star they were overjoyed' (Matthew 2:1–2, 9–10).

The journey and resulting presentation of gold, incense and myrrh to Jesus is celebrated annually at the Feast of the Epiphany on the 6 January. Epiphany comes from a Greek word meaning a sudden realisation or comprehension of the essence or meaning of something. An 'epiphany moment' serves to provide a new experience, often insignificant in itself, which illuminates a foundational truth. In this example of the journey of the three wise men, the epiphany moment for them was the realisation of the divinity of the Christ child, a realisation no longer confined to a stable but now released to the outside world (i.e. the Gentiles). This babe cradled in a manger was no less than 'a light for revelation to the Gentiles' (Luke 2:32).

The awesome night skies in Africa did not bring me to Christ but moved me from a fixed position of unbelief and stirred a renewed spirit of enquiry in my head and heart. My spiritual journey was given fresh impetus – for which I will be forever grateful.

> 'Lift your eyes and look to the heavens: who created all these?'
>
> *Isaiah 40:26*

VISITING

> 'The white of a smile may be more nourishing than the white of a glass of milk.'
>
> *The Talmud*

Great leaders care about individuals. Towards the end of the Second World War, General Eisenhower spent the last days before the D-Day landings visiting his troops rather than the 'top brass'. He mingled with soldiers about to set foot in Europe, and with sailors and airmen. Of course, Eisenhower was aware he couldn't visit all of them but he knew word would spread that he cared about his men as individuals. He knew too that this would give them the added courage and strength so needed in battle.

Visiting can have great significance yet, sadly, this is often overlooked. It is a curious paradox in this age of social networking, emails and Twitter, when we are in 'contact' with an ever-increasing number of people, that loneliness is a growing problem in communities around the country. For all that technology has enabled in terms of connectivity, it has failed to satisfy the 'face-to-face' relational hunger that resides in the heart of each one of us. Indeed it can never succeed in this. At the beginning of the Creation account, when God said to Adam, 'It is not good for the man to be alone,' he followed up that observation with the words, 'I will make a helper suitable for him' (Genesis 2:18). People have been created – emotionally and physiologically – to live in relationship; we need one another, and paying a visit to others is one way of acknowledging this.

In the course of my time as a church minister, notwithstanding the 'busyness' of each day, I increasingly recognised the importance of this truth. On countless occasions a visit yielded immeasurably more than I could have ever imagined, and revealed God at work in the midst of the encounter. Three contrasting examples serve to illustrate this.

On one occasion I was invited to take the church music group on a visit to Bullingdon Prison, near Oxford, for an evening meeting in the chapel. The group was made up of a number of young adults, most had never previously been inside a prison, and our brief was to lead a time of worship and talk about the love of God. Before we set off we prayed that God would be in the midst of our encounter with the prisoners who joined us (there turned out to be about forty in number) and that we would be given the right words to say to each one.

As the prisoners arrived in the chapel, we greeted

them as they sat down. Some were friendly but a number barely lifted their eyes, and it was clear that most of the prisoners knew little about each other. In the front row sat a huge African. I asked him where he came from and he replied 'Nigeria' (a country I had lived in for three years). Spontaneously, I replied in the one African language I knew slightly: '*Sannu, lafiya? Ina aiki?*' [Hello, how are you? How is your work?] He burst out laughing, grinning from ear to ear, and replied in the same African language, namely Hausa, one of the most widespread of the more than 500 languages spoken in Nigeria. The man was on remand and had been at the prison for three weeks, during which time, according to the officers, he had spoken to no one. Instantly he relaxed and began to mix with those around him.

Another man was from China. The prison officials had had difficulty engaging with him because of his lack of English – he spoke a dialect of Mandarin – and he sat quietly, detached from everyone else. To my incredulity one of the music group, a Dutch girl who was studying in Oxford, was a linguist who fluently spoke the very dialect spoken by the prisoner! In no time they were in deep conversation.

You can perhaps imagine the scene in the chapel that evening as two men, hitherto silent and sullen, felt included. It was if walls had been suddenly broken down, and through the 'unwitting' use of common languages not only were two prisoners deeply moved, the whole gathering was engaged.

In word and song we began to share how God is deeply concerned with individuals and longs to speak to each of us in a 'language' we can understand, sometimes literally (as had just happened) and sometimes metaphorically. By the end of the evening, as we drank coffee with the men before they returned to their cells, many wanted to pray and receive the love of Jesus. None of us would ever forget that visit!

On another occasion, Paul, a student from a nearby theological college came to the parish for his placement and I shared with him my conviction about the importance of visiting in the parish. One afternoon provided just the opportunity and, after praying together for the Lord's guidance, we left the vicarage to visit a recently completed housing complex. Hitherto, I had not paid a visit there and I had no idea how many people had moved in. Sending up arrow prayers as we walked along the pavement, we arrived at the first apartment and pressed the doorbell. No reply.

We moved to the next apartment, pressed the bell and heard movement. More arrow prayers! The door opened and a Pakistani woman appeared, uttering the words we least expected to hear! 'We've been praying for a couple of days that you would visit us.' Apparently Susan and her friend, Gulshan Esther, had been attending services for a short while at St Aldate's Church, in the centre of Oxford, and, following a recent service, had been praying that someone from the parish would visit them in their new home. Just days later, Paul and I knocked on their door!

As we spoke it soon became clear that Gulshan Esther had experienced a most remarkable conversion in Pakistan and that she and her companion, Susan, were exercising a powerful ministry across Europe. (Gulshan Esther's moving and powerful autobiography can be read in two best-selling paperbacks.*)

The consequences of that visit were foundational and far-reaching for the parish, Susan and Esther and, not least, Paul as he prepared to embark upon church leadership. For the parish there was a renewed sense of God at work amid the developments taking place in the community, while Susan and Esther no longer felt isolated from the local Christian community as they travelled far and wide to share the love of God, valuing the prayer support and fellowship offered by their local church. Last, and not least, a minister in training experienced the far-reaching benefits that can flow from a programme of visiting underpinned by prayer.

A further occasion which illustrates the way in which God's hand can be revealed through visiting occurred one Saturday morning. Each Saturday an early morning, pre-breakfast prayer meeting was held at church and one week, as I was preparing for the meeting, I was 'prompted' to reflect on the wonder of blood (all it does inside our bodies) and its place in the

---

* *The Torn Veil* and *Beyond the Veil*, published by Zondervan, USA.

scriptures. An ideal pre-breakfast subject you may be thinking!

In the event the prayer meeting went really well and, afterwards, walking back to the vicarage from the church, I bumped into Rod, a local man who never came to church but who I'd got to know as a neighbour. He asked me whether I had heard that his friend Ron, who was also not a churchgoer, was very ill and had been admitted into the local hospice. This was news to me and I asked him whether Ron would welcome a visit. Rod was positive, and by the time I arrived back at the vicarage I'd resolved to go immediately after breakfast. As I drove to the hospice I prayed that God would be at the heart of my meeting with Ron and that I would be given the right words to say. A remarkable hour was to follow…

When I entered Ron's room he was having a blood transfusion! To 'break the ice' I mentioned that I'd just been at a prayer meeting reflecting upon the wonder of blood. This unexpected link avoided the need for many of the usual preliminaries. Ron nodded and with a smile he began to talk about his connections with the church, as a young lad in the choir, and how despite his non-appearance in the local church, he retained vestiges of a faith in God. As I looked at Ron, facing the reality of his own mortality, I was reminded of the old saying that 'there are very few atheists in the front line'.

Before long he was showing a clear interest in the gospel and it was a profoundly moving moment when, forty-five minutes later, Ron prayed a prayer committing his life to the Lord. The moment he said 'Amen' the door opened and his nurse looked in to check how the transfusion was progressing. Looking at me she said, 'I saw you in church last Sunday!' The evening the nurse was referring to I had been leading a service with several hundred people at St Aldate's church and I had no idea she had been present. I turned to Ron as I was about to leave and said, 'I'll leave you now, Ron, in the hands of your Christian "midwife"!' We all smiled and I returned home, reflecting on the events of that morning, so 'unplanned' yet quite unforgettable.

Ron died two weeks later but, having been restless and ill at ease since entering the hospice, in that final fortnight it was as if he had been bathed in peace (indeed, his visitors commented on this in bewilderment to the nurses) and he died with the hope of Christ in his heart.

The simple truth these three stories reveal is that, again and again, visiting yields the unexpected and can have far-reaching relational consequences. People sometimes ask me 'Why visit?' My reply is that so often 'visiting can have the same effect as rewiring a house with the electricity still on!' It generates sparks, many quite unexpected, which serve to reveal how God, who himself visited this earth, cares for individuals… and, by His Spirit, inhabits the wider community.

'The Word became flesh and made his dwelling among us.'

John 1:14

WEMBLEY CONFERENCE CENTRE

> 'We do not create our destiny; we participate in its unfolding. Synchronicity works as a catalyst towards the working out of that destiny.'
>
> *David Richo*

> 'An anniversary is the celebration of love, trust, partnership, tolerance and tenacity. The order varies in any given year.'
>
> *Paul Sweeney*

Friday was the day of 'Sabbath rest' for us in the parish. Following a number busy days and with a full weekend ahead, Chris and I had some time to ourselves. We were sitting down to a leisurely breakfast when the letterbox rattled as the morning's post was delivered. The thud on the floor told me that the latest edition of the weekly *Watford Observer* had arrived and I could catch up on all the latest news from my beloved football club. This, let the reader understand, was in the ancient era 'BC' – 'before computers', the Internet and websites. The regular weekly read of the *Watford Observer* was my key lifeline to Watford FC, the football club I have supported for decades.

Within a few minutes my already positive mood soared even further, a potential threat to Chris' benign entry into the day. Scanning the back pages – like many men I read the paper from back to front – my eye caught sight of a planned anniversary celebration at the Wembley Conference Centre to mark Watford Football Club's Official Centenary in 1992. A potential fly in the ointment was that it was scheduled for a Sunday evening but, on checking the planned service programme, I realised that on the Sunday in question I was, unusually, free from all obligations by lunchtime. There was unconfined joy on my side of the breakfast table: a resigned sigh from the other side.

So it was that I climbed into the car in the late afternoon on Sunday 3 May and set off up the M40 from Oxford to Wembley Stadium. My heart was full of expectancy. Which of my boyhood heroes from the 50s and 60s would be present? How many would I recognise after the passage of, in some cases, nearly forty years? Which past managers would be attending? Would I recognise any familiar faces among the supporters or backroom staff? How would the evening unfold – introductions, speeches, food, and so on?

In addition, I was wondering what God was planning. I was so grateful that I was free to attend the evening, not least because I have held the well-being of the club in my prayers from the earliest days of becoming a Christian. Supporting the club from a young age, I had not only attended matches but had visited the training ground on occasions and sponsored various pieces of equipment for players over the decades. As a result, friendships with a number of individuals have been established. As I set off for Wembley, I simply prayed that the Lord would bless the evening and enable me to 'keep in step with him'.

The journey was straightforward and, surprisingly, so was parking. Arriving in good time, I strolled into the Conference Centre, followed directions to the Watford FC event and entered the large room where the celebration was being held. Immediately one thing caught my eye – tables were laid out for players from each decade. Excellent! During the meal and speeches I could glance around and give myself time to identify as many faces as possible, recall moments from matches when they had made an impression and then, I hoped, have a conversation or two when the formal part of the evening was over.

The evening began with an excellent meal. Then Lawrie McMenemy, Elton John, Cliff Holton and a number of other dignitaries delivered a series of engaging and amusing speeches and a number of presentations were made. Afterwards the evening became more informal and, over coffee, everyone was able to mingle with one another.

I'd already spoken to David Holdsworth, a player whom I had known since his youth team days, and he now introduced me to one of his fellow defenders, Joe McLaughlin. 'Joe, meet John, an old friend of mine. He's a vicar in Oxford.' As I reached out to shake Joe's hand, I noticed his eyes beginning to water. His wife, Linda, sitting alongside him, was similarly moved. I sat down and, after the usual opening exchanges, I said to Joe and Linda, 'Have you ever been to Oxford?' Their reply opened up a deep, moving conversation.

It transpired that their second son, Andrew, had been born a few years earlier when Joe had been playing for Chelsea. At the time, Joe was going through a tough spell on the pitch, his form was shaky and the supporters were predictably unforgiving. The situation became significantly more challenging for Joe and Linda when it was discovered at Andrew's birth that he had a heart defect that needed immediate attention. At once he was taken to the John Radcliffe hospital in Oxford where sadly, after a few days, he died. Throughout this period, Joe and Linda received little support or understanding from either their football colleagues or, not surprisingly, from the supporters, who had no idea what Joe was facing. Day by day, he was expected to pick himself up and throw himself into the daily demands of training and the fray of first team football. Before long, with form proving elusive, Joe was placed on the transfer list, and attention was focused on finding his successor at Chelsea. Joe and Linda were left to carry their grief alone and, in due time, Joe was transferred to Watford FC.

All this was shared at a table in the midst of a crowded Conference Centre but for Joe, Linda and me it was as if we were in our own private room. Intimate and painful moments were being recalled as Joe reflected that, despite the apparent camaraderie amongst players and staff, relationships in the world of sport are so often shallow and transient.

As they continued to share their story and reveal their deep-lying grief, I reflected silently on the hidden costs of performing on the public stage. Do we ever give due thought to what concerns those we expect to perform at consistently high standards have to deal with in private? Perhaps we should not forget they are human beings, not machines.

Clearly, that evening there was much unfinished business to deal with. If we merely bury painful episodes, as Joe and Linda had tried to do in their struggle to move on, those things continue to burrow away inside us and are liable to emerge later, causing even bigger problems. We agreed it would be good to meet up again and I arranged to visit them at their home.

When we met later and talked through all that had happened, I tried to explain how God had been present through all the darkest moments and that, through prayer, his healing touch and his forgiveness could still deal with all their grief and hurt. By the grace of God,

Joe and Linda came to accept this and, after we'd prayed, they experienced a significant sense of release from the burden they had been carrying. Both of them were able to move on in their lives and Joe continued in coaching roles once his playing days were over.

We have kept in touch at a distance since that time, I continue to pray for them and their family and, when facing subsequent challenges in their lives, both Joe and Linda have discovered in fresh ways the renewing, redeeming power of God in their lives.

Of course, if that *Watford Observer* had not dropped through my letterbox... If I had not been free that Sunday night... If David had not introduced me to Joe... If I had not mentioned Oxford and if God had not been at work, none of this would have ever happened. In that case, three lives – Joe's, Linda's and mine – would have been immeasurably the poorer.

In the years since that Sunday evening encounter in the Wembley Conference Centre, each of us has subsequently reflected upon the gift of God's fingerprints upon the Watford FC anniversary celebration.

> 'Now to him who is able to do immeasurably more than all we ask or could imagine, according to his power that is at work within us, to him be glory in the church and in Christ Jesus throughout all generations, for ever and ever! Amen.'
>
> *Ephesians 3:20–21*

X-RAYS

When did you last have an X-ray taken of some part of your body? Perhaps, like me, you're always fascinated by the picture that emerges and want to look at it. Having never sat in a biology lesson, my knowledge about what's inside me is woefully lacking and I've always been intrigued to see the broken nose/leg/collarbone/tooth cavity in question as well as all the other bits and pieces that show up. Not least it helps me understand why remedial action has to be taken.

As with many scientific discoveries, X-rays were discovered by accident in 1895 by Conrad Roentgen, a German scientist. While he was experimenting with cathode rays late one night in his laboratory, he took a photograph of his wife's hand that clearly revealed her ring and her bones. Her immediate response was to exclaim, 'I have seen my death!' Roentgen termed the new form of radiation 'X' as it was an unknown type – and the name stuck. In Germany, sometimes X-rays are still referred to as Roentgen rays.

X-rays have a very short wavelength and largely pass through skin and muscle to be absorbed by the denser bones (including teeth) and any metal within a body. They are widely used in airport security, at border controls and in engineering to test welding. One of the greatest contributions they have made to the medical world is to enable doctors to 'see' inside us and examine broken bones and other organs without having to operate, thus greatly reducing the risk of infection. Without X-rays our provision of health care and national security would be severely compromised.

Knowing as much as possible about what's going on out of sight, whether inside our bodies or at our national borders, is so important if we are to remain healthy and secure – a truth we would do well to remember in a culture obsessed with outward appearance. Appearances can be very misleading.

Appearance is, of course, important – and dressing appropriately is not to be dismissed, as my wife constantly reminds me! The desire to feel a sense of belonging and acceptance in any gathering is understandable, as has been recognised in every culture throughout human history. However, given the powerful hold that the media and fashion industry have assumed in society today, it is important to be reminded that appearance isn't everything.

Being unduly influenced by appearances is nothing new. The Old Testament records the time when the prophet Samuel went to Bethlehem to choose a new king of Israel. The Lord had said to Samuel he was to choose a king from one of the sons of Jesse, and when he arrived in Bethlehem:

'Samuel saw Eliab [Jesse's oldest son] and thought, "Surely the Lord's anointed stands here before the Lord."

'But the Lord said to Samuel, "Do not consider his appearance or his height, for I have rejected him. The Lord does not look at the things man looks at. Man looks at the outward appearance, but the Lord looks at the heart"' (1 Samuel 16:6–7).

In the New Testament there is another reminder that 'God does not judge by external appearance' (Galatians 2:6) when Jesus, in his denunciation of the scribes and the Pharisees, declares, 'Woe to you, teachers of the law and Pharisees, you hypocrites! You are like whitewashed tombs which look beautiful on the outside but on the inside are full of dead men's bones and everything unclean. In the same way, on the outside you appear to people as righteous but on the inside you are full of hypocrisy and wickedness' (Matthew 23:27,28).

'Don't judge a book by its cover' is an old maxim but it applies to the perspective God has when he looks at us – with eyes that are like X-rays. God sees 'through' us because he longs for each of us to become fully human, to be fully alive. We need to become people of integrity and God, who created us, knows this.

When we open our hearts to the Holy Spirit, Jesus tells us the first thing the Spirit does is to 'convict us of [our] guilt in regard to sin' (John 16:8). This is not because God wants to condemn us but rather because he longs to set us free from carrying the weight of guilt around, for he knows what a burden that is. He wants to heal us through and through. As we ask forgiveness for the sins that are identified, so the burden of them is released. This transformation is invariably an ongoing process as we are 'transformed into his likeness with ever-increasing glory' (2 Corinthians 3:18).

For me, the first thing God put his finger on when I opened my life to him was my language. Having inhabited men's culture through sport, university and casual labour, my use of swear words was frequent and unthinking. When the Spirit entered my heart I was immediately convicted of this error of my ways and, while I cannot say I have never let an expletive pass my lips since then, the truth is that my use of language has been transformed, and I have found that liberating.

That sense of liberation which comes from being set free from bad habits is beautifully expressed by the psalmist David in one of the many psalms he wrote:

> Blessed is he whose transgressions are forgiven,
>   whose sins are covered.
> Blessed is the man whose sin the Lord does not
>   count against him and in whose spirit is no
>   deceit.

When I kept silent my bones wasted away through
    my groaning all day long.
For day and night your hand was heavy upon me; my
    strength was sapped as in the heat of summer.
Then I acknowledged my sin before you and did
    not cover up my iniquity.
I said, "I will confess my transgressions to the
    Lord" – and you forgave the guilt of my sin.

Psalm 32:1–5

God's forgiveness and inner healing are so precious. They came at great cost to God, yet are offered freely to each of us through his mercy and grace, as we place our faith in Jesus Christ. Some find the acronym <u>G</u>od's <u>R</u>iches <u>A</u>t <u>C</u>hrist's <u>E</u>xpense a helpful way to remember the deep, deep significance of 'grace'.

Just as X-rays offer us a path to healing and security in our daily lives, so too do the 'X-ray eyes of God'.

'You have searched me, Lord, and you know me…
Search me, God, and know my heart; test me and
know my anxious thoughts. See if there is any offensive
way in me, and lead me in the way everlasting.'

Psalm 139: 1, 23–24

YACHTS AND AUTUMN LEAVES

'I can't change the direction of the wind, but I can adjust my sails to always reach my destination.'

Jimmy Dean

On the morning of the finals at the 1973 National Sailing Championships in Bombay, India, the sun rose to reveal a beautiful sailing day with a steady wind blowing. Pre-race tensions were running high as the competitors negotiated their way to the start line; each yacht seeking to gain an advantage over its rivals from the moment the starting gun was fired. One of the sailors, George Kavoor, reflecting on those final minutes, recalls: 'I approached the start line on my own from the other side to the rest of the fleet and so was on my own for most of the race. I therefore charted my own course without reference to anyone else. I won the race with a lead of at least twenty minutes.'

To choose a different route from everybody else at

such a prestigious event took great courage. Having made his own assessment – based on calculations of wind speed and direction, coupled with the published weather forecast for the period of the race – George was backing his own judgement. Unlike every other competitor seeking to win the prize, he was prepared to 'stand out from the crowd'.

Meanwhile, back on the streets of Oxford, England, some days Terry was a happy man, some days he was a bit grumpy – it all depended on the wind and the season of the year. Terry was the local road sweeper, a popular figure who quietly and faithfully swept the roads for many years. Often, in the late autumn, he would arrive in the parish for a day's work and be confronted with a dispiriting scene – countless numbers of fallen leaves swirling in the wind, filling gutters, blocking drains and offering the prospect of many, many barrow loads to be swept up and carried off. I would commiserate with him as I passed him in the street and Terry would respond with a smile and a shrug of the shoulders.

Impressed with his fortitude, I was doubly impressed to discover that a week or two later the trees would be almost bare yet there was scarcely a leaf in sight on the streets! When I congratulated him on his work, Terry simply shrugged his shoulders and said 'I didn't do it all alone, you know.' As we chatted he explained that no, he didn't have an army of helpers to call upon, but he had discovered that if he waited, the wind and rain collected the leaves at certain convenient points and this allowed him to put each pile in his cart. Result? Terry's work was productive and satisfying and the community he served was profoundly grateful!

Both these stories, one recounting a prestigious national yachting final and the other recalling a humble road sweeper on the streets of Oxford, offer the same great lesson – the importance of deciding to work co-operatively with the wind, a decision that can require both courage and patience.

Because of my interest in meteorology, having studied it at university, I was intrigued to discover that wind is one of the foremost images used to refer to God's Spirit in the Bible. In the Old Testament, written in Hebrew, the word used is '*ruach*' and in the New Testament, written in Greek, the word is '*pneuma*'. Jesus, when he speaks to Nicodemus about the importance of being 'born again', says:

'I tell you the truth, no one can enter the kingdom of God unless he is born of water and the Spirit. Flesh gives birth to flesh, but the Spirit gives birth to spirit. You should not be surprised at my saying, "You must be born again." The wind blows wherever it pleases. You hear its sound, but you cannot tell where it comes from or where it is going. So it is with everyone born of the Spirit' (John 3:5–8).

The image he uses of the wind is simply a way of picturing the Spirit's unpredictability, invisibility and power. Although Jesus refers to the wind as 'it', the language used of the Holy Spirit is always personal, using personal pronouns 'his', 'him' and 'he', because he is recognised as a personal being in the Bible – the third member of the Trinity, together with the Father and Jesus.

Both Terry and George Kavoor discovered the wisdom and benefits of working co-operatively with the wind in order to succeed in their goals and, if we are to discover life in all its fullness (and who doesn't want that?), we need to work co-operatively with the Holy Spirit. Just as the wind does not seize control over us, neither does the Spirit. He doesn't want to overwhelm us but to work within and alongside us. He longs to show us the ways of God and point us to Jesus, help us to understand God's Word, strengthen us, encourage us, release creativity within us and to change each of us to become more fully the person we were created to be. In short, the Holy Spirit seeks to make us 'fully alive', at our invitation – he never wants to be a dictator.

This process of transformation, aided by the Spirit, is not a 'one-off' experience but a gradual process of changes that can span a lifetime. By one degree after another we 'are being transformed into his likeness with ever-increasing glory, which comes from the Lord, who is the Spirit' (2 Corinthians 3:18). Just as we regularly need to exercise and take in the air we breathe, if this work of transformation is to continue we need to 'go on being filled with the Spirit' (Ephesians 3:18).

At no point in their lives did Terry, as he swept up the leaves, or George Kavoor, as he sailed over the water, conclude that they could ignore the wind if they were to achieve their goals. Neither can we ignore the wind of the Spirit if we are to achieve our goal in life to become more fully alive – the transforming, energising, creative, loving work of the Holy Spirit who longs to bestow on us 'life in all its fullness'.

Come, Holy Spirit. Amen.

'Create in me a pure heart, O God, and renew a steadfast spirit within me.'

Psalm 51:10

ZOE – WHAT'S IN A NAME?

> 'Names are an important key to what a society values. Anthropologists recognise naming as one of the chief methods for imposing order on perception... People pay greater attention to things that have been given names.'
>
> *David S. Slawson*

What's in a name?

I discovered to my cost the answer to this question when I was a school teacher. One day an economics teacher decided to give his sixth form class a free period just before lunch and one of his students, having no outstanding work to complete, sat down in the library and wondered how he should fill his time. Straight ahead of him on one of the shelves he saw a copy of *A Dictionary of English Surnames* and decided to spend the time looking up the origins of various teachers' surnames. Cook, Smith, Cooper... one by one he worked his way through the staff and then thought, 'I bet old Samways' name isn't in this book.' He turned the pages and to his surprise he found it was there. Within a moment his surprise turned into barely contained delight as he read the following entry:

Samways – derived from the old English, meaning 'semi-wise', probable origin 'village idiot'.

At a conservative estimate, within half an hour of the ensuing lunch break that sweet morsel of information had spread through the whole school community. Any semblance of authority I had previously enjoyed or imagined evaporated in an instant!

So often a name is more than merely a label, more than a random combination of sounds. A name can convey nature, history or reputation; indeed a person's reputation is referred to as his 'good name'.

There are examples of this concept on more than one occasion in the Bible. When God speaks to his servant Abram he says, 'No longer will you be called Abram; your name will be Abraham, for I have made you the father of many nations' (Genesis 17:5). The name Abram means 'exalted father', Abraham means 'father of many'; the significance of this change of name was that the Lord had just appeared to Abram, aged ninety-nine years, and told him his wife, Sarah, who was herself aged ninety, was shortly to give birth to a son whom he was to name Isaac. The name Isaac means 'he laughs', a reminder of the moment when Abram laughed (Genesis 17:17) at the thought that he would be a father aged one hundred years!

In Matthew's Gospel account of the birth of Jesus, he records the moment an angel appeared to Joseph in a dream and said, 'Joseph, son of David, do not be afraid to take Mary home as your wife, because what is conceived in her is from the Holy Spirit. She will give birth to a son, and you are to give him the name Jesus, because he will save his people from their sins' (Matthew 1:20, 21). Clearly the name had deep significance, for Jesus means 'saviour' and indicates that the purpose of Jesus' life was for him to come and 'give his life as a ransom for many' (Mark 10:45).

In the course of his ministry, at a time when Jesus was talking to those who were questioning his ministry among the crowds that followed him, he said, 'I have come that you might have life – life in all its fullness' (John 10:10, Good News Translation). John recorded these words of Jesus in his Gospel, which he wrote in Greek, a language in which there are two words for life, namely '*bios*' and '*zoe*'. The word *bios* appears frequently as a prefix in the English language, in words such as *bio*logy, *bio*graphy, *bio*chemistry and *bio*sphere. Each of these words refer in some way to 'life' – in short, every living thing possesses *bios* life, every human being, every animal, every plant. However, the life Jesus seeks to bring to this world is not merely *bios* life but a new dimension of life, namely 'life in all its fullness'. To signify this different dimension of life, John does not use *bios* but *zoe*. He recognises that Jesus longs for each and every one of us to discover and receive *zoe* life – a life that is spiritually alive and rooted in a new, dynamic, living relationship with God. Indeed it is clear that John wrote his Gospel account in order to bring his readers to faith in Jesus Christ: 'Jesus did many other miraculous signs in the presence of his disciples, which are not recorded in this book. But these are written that you may believe that Jesus is the Christ, the Son of God, and that by believing you may have life [*zoe*] in his name' (John 20:30,31).

One night Nicodemus, a member of the Jewish ruling council who was trying to get his head around what Jesus was saying and doing, went to see Jesus who said to him, 'I tell you the truth, no one can see the kingdom of God, unless he is born again' (John 3:3). Jesus goes on to explain that everyone needs to be 'born of the Spirit'; it is not our natural birth that marks our becoming a child of God but the moment when we open our hearts to God's Spirit through faith in Jesus Christ. That is the moment we are transformed from mere *bios* life to *zoe* life, the moment when the saving work of Jesus through his death on the Cross becomes a living reality to us and we enter into 'eternal life'. The significance of this is clearly explained in the following verses as John's Gospel unfolds:

'For God so loved the world that he gave his one and only Son, that whoever believes in him shall not perish but have eternal life' (John 3:16).

'Whoever believes in the Son has eternal life, but whoever rejects the Son will not see life, for God's wrath remains on him' (John 3:36).

'I tell you the truth, whoever hears my word and believes him who sent me has eternal life and will not be condemned; he has passed over from death to life' (John 5:24).

'Now this is eternal life: that they may know you, the only true God, and Jesus Christ, whom you have sent' (John 17:3).

Do you know anyone with the name of *Zoe*? Does she know the significance of her name?

The eighteenth-century hymn writer Charles Wesley, who with his brother John founded the Methodist movement, wrote over 6,000 hymns, many of which are now long forgotten. However, one that has endured and stamped itself deep into Methodism and is regularly sung today is 'Jesus the name high over all'. This hymn captures memorably the power and authority that reside in the name of the One who came that we might have life (*zoe*) and have it to the full.

> Jesus the name to sinners dear,
> the name to sinners given;
> it scatters all their guilty fear,
> it turns their hell to heaven.
>
> *Charles Wesley, 1749*

At about the same time as Wesley wrote this hymn, John

Newton was a slave trader with a particularly fearsome reputation. Slaves being carried from Africa to America suffered cruelly at his hands until, in 1748 when he was on a merchant ship sailing near Donegal, Newton experienced a spiritual conversion. In the following years, with *zoe* life flowing through his veins, he abandoned drinking and gambling, his language changed dramatically and he began to study the Bible in Greek and Hebrew. In due time he became a lay minister and finally was ordained in 1764, and it was John Newton who penned a hymn that so graphically captures the significance of the name of Jesus:

> How sweet the name of Jesus sounds
> in a believer's ear;
> It soothes his sorrows, heals his wounds,
> drives away his fears.

John Newton, 1779

What's in a name? It's certainly worth investigating!

> 'Therefore God exalted him to the highest place and gave him the name that is above every name, that at the name of Jesus every knee should bow, in heaven and on earth and under the earth, and every tongue confess that Jesus Christ is Lord to the glory of God the Father.'
>
> *Philippians 2:9–11*

I am... JESUS

'He changed sunset into sunrise.'

Clement of Alexander

If you read the first Jesus entry earlier in this book you may have wondered why I decided to move the main entry for Jesus here. It was as a result of reflecting on the verse 'The word became flesh and lived for a while among us' (John 1:14). When Jesus was born, God's fingerprints touched this earth for over thirty years so (given the theme of this book) it seems appropriate to let him 'have the last word'.

Jesus had a habit of asking important questions. One of the most important he presented to his disciples was, 'Who do you say that I am?' (Matthew 16:13) and this question remains perhaps the most important question facing each of us today. Who was Jesus? What was he about? Why should we care two thousand years later?

Few scholars question the existence of Jesus as a historical figure. Indeed, two significant historians of the first century, the Jewish writer Josephus and the

Roman senator and historian Tacitus, both refer to Jesus and the origins of Christianity in their writings, although neither was a follower of Jesus. But who exactly was this man – this wandering peasant; this outrageous, unorthodox rebellious teacher and miracle worker who hung out with doubtful characters; this man who was beaten, bloodied, spat upon and 'killed' with common criminals? Could it be that the baby born in a stable, in an obscure village in Palestine 2,000 years ago, is God incarnate? Could Jesus be the one promised by the prophet Isaiah when he declared 'the people living in darkness have seen a great light; on those living in the land of the shadow of death a light has dawned' (Isaiah 9:1,2)? Is he 'the Christ, the Son of the living God' (Matthew 16:16)? And if he *were*, what would be the significance of that for us today?

It seems that when John sat down to write his gospel account, he had one overriding aim in mind – *to answer these very questions.* As he draws to a conclusion he writes, 'Jesus did many other miraculous signs in the presence of his disciples which are not recorded in this book. But these are written that you may believe that Jesus is the Christ, the Son of God, and that in believing you may have life in his name' (John 20:30, 31).

In his Gospel, John records a series of famous 'I am' sayings, a number of which are quite familiar to many people, such as 'I am the good shepherd' and 'I am the light of the world'. These word pictures give us a revealing insight as to how Jesus answers his own question 'Who do you say that I am?' A closer look at each one, seeing what it communicates, can help us as we seek to respond to Jesus' question ourselves.

It is important to understand that when Jesus used these 'I am' sayings, the Jews of the time would have understood he was claiming to be God. In one conversation, when he was being challenged about who he was and his claim to have seen Abraham, Jesus replies, 'I tell you the truth, before Abraham was born, I am' (John 8:58). Immediately his hearers would have linked these words with the moment when Moses met God in the burning bush and, when asked his name, God said to Moses, 'I am who I am. This is what you are to say to the Israelites: "I AM has sent me to you"' (Exodus 3:14).

Clearly the 'I am' sayings were intended as word portraits of what God is doing as well as Jesus, for as has been aptly said, 'Jesus is the best photograph of God ever taken'. So let's take a walk through the Jesus 'portrait' gallery.

'I am the bread of life'
The first 'I am' saying in John's Gospel is 'I am the bread of life. He who comes to me will never go hungry…' (John 6:35). In first century Palestine, bread was the staple diet of the common people – it was the sustenance for life – and the sound of millstones would be heard daily in every village. If this noise ceased even for a day it was the sign of no more bread: nothing to

eat. Jeremiah uses an ominous picture when prophesying the Lord's judgement, declaring the Lord will 'banish from them … the sound of millstones' (Jeremiah 25:10).

Clearly, bread has to be consumed to provide nourishment: the implication in this word picture is that the bread of heaven has to be accepted and be made part of our being to nourish us. Jesus goes on to say, 'I am the living bread that came down from heaven. If anyone eats of this bread, he will live forever. This bread is my flesh, which I will give for the life of the world' (John 6:51). In this word portrait, Jesus identifies himself as an essential part of the 'diet' of his hearers, that he is willing to give himself up for others. How fitting, incidentally, that the phrase comes from the lips of one born in Bethlehem (literally 'House of Bread')! We need to see past the bread to the food, past the food to the message, and through the message to the significance of Jesus.

'I am the light of the world'

The second word portrait in the gallery is associated with another essential to all life – light. The first spoken words of God in creation were 'Let there be light' (Genesis 1:2), and light appeared. Sadly, as our daily headlines remind us, the lives of so many today are spent in darkness, whether literal or metaphorical. No one is completely at home in the dark, although people can learn to accustom themselves to living with light from candles, torches, light bulbs or fires. Light reveals colour, beauty, dangers, pathways and perspective. Light also encourages growth and is fundamental to life. When Jesus said, 'I am the light of the world. Whoever follows me will never walk in darkness, but will have the light of life' (John 8:12), it is little wonder he was challenged by the Jewish religious authorities – for they recognised this statement was an indictment of their own leadership. This sparked a robust debate among them, which came to an abrupt end when 'they picked up stones to stone him' (John 8:59).

These first two portraits were shared with the crowds of ordinary people that gathered around Jesus; subsequent portraits are more focused.

'I am the good shepherd'

Following Jesus' healing of a blind man (John 9), the religious leaders rejected the man's account of his healing and threw him out of the synagogue. It was to these self-appointed leaders of the synagogue that Jesus declared, 'I am the good shepherd. The good shepherd lays down his life for the sheep' (John 10:11).

In the Old Testament, God is seen as the Shepherd of Israel (Psalm 80:1), a role assigned to the priests. Through the prophet Jeremiah, God makes clear that the priests are failing in their duties when he declares, 'Woe to the shepherds who are destroying and scattering the sheep of my pasture!' (Jeremiah 23:1). It is from this perspective that Jesus rebukes the Pharisees as he unpacks this word portrait (*see* John 10:11–18). A good shepherd does not abandon his flock, he knows his flock and they know him, they recognise and listen to his voice. Rather than scattering the flock, a good shepherd protects it, keeps it together and seeks to draw other sheep into it. More than that, a good shepherd is even prepared to lay down his life for the sheep rather than abandoning them in the face of danger.

'I am the gate for the sheep'

One of the ways shepherds used to protect their flocks at night was to sleep across the entrance to the sheepfold, thus guarding against thieves and predators entering the fold and ensuring the flock did not wander off and get lost. Thus Jesus said, 'I tell you the truth, I am the gate for the sheep' (John 10:7).

Quite simply, the desire of the good shepherd is that his flock 'may have life, and have it to the full' (John 10:10). This pastoral picture and its implications would immediately have been appreciated by those drawn to this itinerant speaker wandering around Galilee, and its implicit criticism would have been recognised by those religious leaders who were failing in their duties.

From this point on in John's Gospel, as his arrival in Jerusalem draws near, Jesus spends more and more of his time with the disciples gathered around him – not the crowds nor the critical religious authorities – but those he was teaching. The 'I am' sayings he now uses become more and more specific to his unique ministry.

'I am the resurrection and the life'

Soon word reaches Jesus that one of his close friends, Lazarus, is sick in Bethany, a village less than two miles from Jerusalem. Rather than rushing to his sick bed, Jesus waits a couple of days and when he finally arrives at the village, Martha, one of Lazarus' sisters, comes out to meet Jesus and declares Lazarus has been dead for four days.

> Jesus said to her, 'Your brother will rise again.' Martha answered, 'I know he will rise again in the resurrection at the last day.' Jesus said to her, 'I am the resurrection and the life. He who believes in me will live, even though he dies; and whoever lives and believes in me will never die. Do you believe this?' 'Yes, Lord,' she told him, 'I believe you are the Christ, the Son of God, who was to come into the world.'
>
> *John 11:23-27*

The powerful impact of these words is extraordinary and their truth is underlined as the story unfolds. After all, if God can raise a decaying corpse then there is no limit to what he can do. Having arrived in Bethany when Lazarus was known to be 'dead and buried' (so no one was in any doubt about this), Jesus finally visits the cave where the body of Lazarus has been entombed. One can scarcely imagine the reaction of onlookers as '…The dead man came out, his hands and feet wrapped with strips of linen, and a cloth round his face, and…

Jesus [says] to them, "Take off the grave clothes and let him go"' (John 11:44).

Jesus' question to Martha at the heart of this account, 'Do you believe this?' makes clear the essential part that faith, faith in a known person, plays in this story. Jesus is declaring that through faith in him there is life – to the full – after death as well as before death (*see* John 10:10). It is important to understand that in the Greek language, in which John writes his Gospel, two words are used for life – *'bios'* and *'zoe'*; whenever John is talking about the life associated with Jesus he uses the word *zoe*. (For more about this see *Zoe – What's in a Name?*)

There is no doubting the central importance of resurrection to the Christian faith. 'If Christ has not been raised [from the dead], our preaching is useless and so is your faith' (1 Corinthians 15:14) writes the apostle Paul. And then to underline the point he adds, 'If Christ has not been raised, your faith is futile' (1 Corinthians 15:17). No wriggle room there, then!

By now it was only six days before the Passover festival, one of the most important festivals of the Jewish year. The time was drawing close to the defining moments in Jesus' life and the scene in John's Gospel soon shifts to the final meal Jesus shared with the disciples before his death on the cross, namely 'the Last Supper' in the Upper Room. It is at this meal, as the table talk continues, that Jesus gives a further word portrait to his closest friends.

'I am the way, the truth and the life'

As Jesus shares how the story is going to unfold in the coming hours, it is not difficult to imagine the growing tension and anxiety in the hearts of the disciples as they contemplate the anticipated loss of their Lord, their hopes shattered and the uncertainty of their future.

Jesus seeks to comfort them with words that are familiar at funeral services today. 'Do not let your hearts be troubled. Trust in God; trust also in me. In my Father's house are many rooms; if it were not so, I would have told you. I am going there to prepare a place for you. And if I go and prepare a place for you, I will come back and take you to be with me that you may also be where I am. You know the way to the place where I am going' (John 14:1–4). The term 'my Father's house' evokes the presence of God, the home of God, heaven itself. Jesus is giving his disciples no less than a perspective beyond death into the promise of eternity – a perspective that is carried to all who hear today.

It is at this point that the disciple Thomas asks the question which, if we are honest, lies in our own hearts as we contemplate the reality of death and the uncertainty of what lies beyond that inevitable moment. 'Lord, we don't know where you are going, so how can we know the way?' (John 14:5). Given the fact that Jesus had just told his disciples, 'Where I am going, you cannot come' (John 13:33), it is little wonder that there was some confusion in the ranks.

Jesus responds to Thomas with a statement that lies

at the very heart of Christian belief: 'I am the way, the truth and the life. No one comes to the Father except through me' (John 14:6). Jesus is stating unequivocally that in him is found the way to God, the truth about God and the life of God. He does not merely show us *a* way to God, he is *the* way and he alone leads us to God. Hence, early Christians were known as 'followers of the Way'.

Similarly, Jesus doesn't merely tell us *a* truth, he exemplifies *the* truth about God: he is 'the exact representation of his being' (Hebrews 1:3). That is why he can state with confidence that 'anyone who has seen me has seen the Father' (John 14:9).

At the very beginning of his Gospel, John writes, 'In him was life, and that life was the light of men' (John 1:4). John is stating more than the fact that Jesus was alive but that he is the true source of all life; he has the gift of life, life in all its fullness, life that transcends death (John 3:36, John 5:21, 24–26). In stating 'I am the life', Jesus is declaring he is the creator and sustainer of *zoe* – he is the true 'life-giver'.

This claim of Jesus, to be *the* way, *the* truth, *the* life is staggering. He is not one among many but unique in who he is and what he offers. Those words were not universally popular when he uttered them, hence his death on a cross some hours later, nor are they today in a world that demands toleration for all viewpoints. Nonetheless, the implication is that, whatever people discover about God through his 'fingerprints' in creation and daily life (and, as the stories in this book show, there are many such discoveries to be made), the search for the way to God, the truth about God and people's hunger for life in all its fullness is only fully realised through faith in Jesus Christ. This is a faith that requires more than mere passing assent to the person of Jesus but an acknowledgement that his rightful place is as Lord of every part of life: 'In your hearts set apart Christ as Lord' (1 Peter 3:15).

What was going through the minds of the disciples at this time? One can only imagine the turmoil in their minds as they endeavoured to digest the significance of all they were hearing! Finally the time came to go, and the group left the Upper Room to begin the walk through the narrow streets of Jerusalem to the Garden of Gethsemane.

'I am the vine'
As the conversation continues, Jesus begins to unpack the intimacy of the relationship that lies at the heart of knowing God and being known by God. He uses an image that had long been familiar to all people in that region, both Jews and Gentiles. He chooses a symbol that is tender, simple and accessible for everyone, namely the vine. Jesus states, 'I am the true vine' (John 15:1) and he uses this image to underline the crucial importance of his followers being intimately associated with him. 'I am the vine; you are the branches. If a man remains in me and I in him, he will bear much fruit; apart from me you can do nothing' (John 15:5).

Jesus develops the picture by saying if we are not linked to him we are like branches being cut off from a living vine, destined to wither and be destroyed. The severe and uncompromising tone of this picture is balanced by the hope, love and fruitful life that is set before those 'branches' that remain attached to the vine, an attachment that is offered as a gift, through faith in him.

Repeatedly through the 'I am' sayings, Jesus is hinting at the crucial significance of relationship – the bread that needs to be consumed, the light that guides, the shepherd and door which protect, the resurrection which brings life out of death, and now the vine which supports, sustains and nourishes its branches in order that they will be fruitful. Passing from one picture to another in sequence is so enlightening in our search to know God and to be known by him. The different facets of each 'I am' saying collectively encourage us on our spiritual journey and that, of course, is why John includes them in his Gospel account. Remember, the gospel was 'written that you may believe that Jesus is the Christ, the Son of God, and that by believing you may have life in his name' (John 20:31).

'I am the alpha and the omega'

Was the John the gospel writer that same John who wrote the final book of the Bible? There is an ongoing debate about this, but it is intriguing to note that the final 'I am' saying recorded in the Bible comes just before the very end of Revelation, the final book in the Bible.

Revelation does not offer additional information about the life of faith in Christ – that is to be found in the other 65 books of the Bible. What this book seeks to do is stir up our imagination, to enable us to see the truth about Jesus revealed in the rest of the Bible in a fresh, coherent way. Revelation is a message communicated from Jesus through an angel to John, a prisoner on the island of Patmos. The message, containing a series of vivid, bizarre and often bewildering visions which are designed to awaken the imagination, is explained in an illuminating way by the American pastor/scholar Eugene Peterson in his book *Reversed Thunder*.

Peterson reflects that people have a deep need for 'intelligible ends', a desire to join their beginning to their ending, and this need is addressed in the final word portrait located in the last chapter of the Bible. God identifies himself with the words: 'I am the Alpha and the Omega, the First and the Last, the Beginning and the End' (Revelation 22:13). All the 'I am' sayings of Jesus are wrapped up in this final picture. Alpha and Omega are the first and last letters of the Greek alphabet – 'God is all the letters of the alphabet'.*

Jesus is identified as the Alpha, the creative

---

*From *Reversed Thunder, the Revelation of John and the Praying Imagination*: Eugene H. Petersen, HarperCollins, New York 1991.

presence of God, present at the beginning of everything, the source of all, on whom we depend for our very existence. 'Through him all things were made; without him nothing was made that has been made. In him was life and that life was the light of mankind' (John 1:3, 4). He is also the Omega, the goal towards which everything is directed; the one in whom people find meaning, hope, and purpose; the one in whom all God's promises find their 'Yes' (2 Corinthians 1:20). It was commonplace in rabbinic meditation on God's name, 'I AM' (Exodus 3:14) to note that God's being embraces all the tenses of the verb 'to be': present, past and future. This is illustrated by John when he describes God as he 'who *is* and who *was* and who *is to come*' (Revelation 1:4, 8), not an easy idea to grasp.

To help us, John uses two Greek words for time, '*chronos*' and '*kairos*'. *Chronos* relates to the time we live in and measure with clocks and calendars. It is related to the earth's orbit and rotation. *Kairos* time involves the motion of heart and mind, and it relates to moments when time 'stands still', moments to cherish. *Kairos* intersects with *chronos* and never leaves us the same. For instance, a holiday or a wedding embraces both *chronos* (dates in the diary, flights, trips etc.) and *kairos* moments (such as an amazing view or encounter). Parenting also embraces both, for example 'I'm having a lovely time playing with you. I wonder how many minutes it will be before Daddy comes home?'

The vital significance of this perspective of *kairos* transecting *chronos* time is that it transforms daily life. Awakened within us, through the gift of the Holy Spirit, is a new awareness of the living presence of God, the one who is past, present and future. This is rooted in the understanding of the present significance of what God *has* accomplished through Jesus and delivers a new anticipation of and expectation in the hope of the future. 'Everything that God is and everything God has been is present, immediate, invading the here and now. Nothing is too remote, either in the distant past or in the far-flung future. In God, past and future impinge, constantly, on the present.'*

This holds true for every square inch of the planet because, shortly after his resurrection, Jesus ascended 'in order to fill the whole universe' (Ephesians 4:10). Wherever we are, our deep need for 'intelligible ends' is found uniquely and comprehensively through faith in the Alpha and the Omega – the risen ascended Jesus Christ.

The following passage provides one of the greatest descriptions summarising his significance. These words are found in the letter the apostle Paul wrote to the church at Colossae, a group of believers who were in danger of drifting away from the truth. It would be time well spent reflecting on how this passage resonates with the 'I am' sayings of Jesus… and with the stories in this book:

---

*From *Reversed Thunder, the Revelation of John and the Praying Imagination*: Eugene H. Petersen. Ibid.

[The Son] is the image of the invisible God, the firstborn over all creation. For by him all things were created: things in heaven and on earth, visible and invisible, whether thrones or powers or rulers or authorities; all things have been created by him and for him. He is before all things, and in him all things hold together. And he is the head of the body, the church; he is the beginning and the firstborn from among the dead, so that in everything he might have the supremacy. For God was pleased to have all his fullness dwell in him, and through him to reconcile to himself all things, whether things on earth or things in heaven, by making peace through his blood, shed on the cross.

Once you were alienated from God and were enemies in your minds because of your evil behaviour. But now he has reconciled you by Christ's physical body through death to present you holy in his sight, without blemish and free from accusation – if you continue in your faith, established and firm, and do not move from the hope held out in the gospel. This is the gospel that you heard and that has been proclaimed to every creature under heaven, and of which I, Paul, have become a servant.

Colossians 1:15-23

It is difficult to imagine a more appropriate place to conclude our journey through the 'I am' portrait gallery. Reflecting on each of the 'I am' sayings of Jesus can help us to see how we can recognise God's 'fingerprints' in the rough and tumble of daily life; each of these word portraits also serves to reveal the deeper significance of stories in this book. Just as no single 'I am' saying of Jesus presents a complete picture of who he is, neither does any one story in this book provide a complete understanding of God and his ways – after all, fingerprints only provide a representative fraction of the whole being they represent. However, just as the 'I am' sayings complement one another and collectively build a more complete picture of who Jesus is and how he acted, so too, the stories in this book show how God continues to act in people's lives today.

Just as Jesus uses figurative language to describe himself as 'a good shepherd', 'light', 'Alpha and Omega' … the term 'God's fingerprints' is, of course, largely figurative. However, it is intriguing to ponder that when 'the Word became flesh and lived for a while among us' (John 1:14), God's fingerprints literally were placed over a small area of Roman-occupied Palestine for thirty-three years!

We live on a visited planet.

> 'That which was from the beginning, which we have heard, which we have seen with our eyes, which we have looked at and our hands have touched – this we proclaim concerning the Word of life. The life appeared, we have seen it and testify to it, and we proclaim to you the eternal life, which was with the Father and has appeared to us. We proclaim to you what we have seen and heard.'
>
> I John I: I–3